Preaching the Gospel

Henry J. Young
editor

with contributions by

William Holmes Borders
Roy C. Nichols
Herbert Bell Shaw
Andrew Young
James H. Cone
Charles B. Copher
A. Roger Williams
Benjamin E. Mays
Martin Luther King, Jr.

Martin Luther King, Sr.
Joseph A. Johnson, Jr.
Henry H. Mitchell
John T. Walker
J. Deotis Roberts, Sr.
William V. Guy
Leon H. Sullivan
Herbert O. Edwards, Sr.
Charles E. Blake

Oswald P. Bronson

FORTRESS PRESS   **Philadelphia**

To my wife, Aleta Joyce
and
my daughter, Aleta Renée

Biblical quotations from the Revised Standard Version of the Bible,
copyrighted 1946, 1952, © 1971, 1973 by the Division of Christian
Education of the National Council of the Churches of Christ in the
U.S.A., are used by permission.

Library of Congress Catalog Card Number 75-36449

ISBN 0-8006-1223-X   NOV 13, 1976

5404B76   Printed in U.S.A.   1-1223

PREFACE

This book brings together nineteen sermons by contemporary black preachers in an attempt to demonstrate the uniqueness, quality, and organic orientation that marks authentic black preaching. Both historically and to the present day black preaching has been organic in that it has appropriated the theological motifs of the Christian faith in light of the social, political, economic, and religious conditions affecting the black community and the nation at large. These sermons do not compartmentalize reality. They do not separate spiritual liberation from physical liberation. They view the salvation of mankind as being inextricably interwoven with man's capacity, by the help of God, to eradicate social evils and to transform the social, political, and economic structures of society.

The contributors to this volume speak out of their own unique experience. This locates their proclamation of the gospel in existential particularity. Accordingly they are concerned with the freedom and liberation of the oppressed, afflicted, enslaved, and persecuted black people of America. At the same time, they are also concerned with the ultimate freedom and redemption of all mankind. Hence the dimension of universality in their preaching. These sermons speak to both black and white communities. The black community has a mandate from God to continue the journey toward freedom and liberation, and the white community must realize that destructive polarization in America and throughout the world will not cease until racism, injustice, oppression, enslavement, and affliction are eradicated.

There is a unity to these sermons in the way they view the gospel. Their understanding of the gospel goes against the distorted view many historians, sociologists, theologians, and anthropologists have had of black preaching. This distorted view has argued that black preaching tends to be without content, passive, an escape mechanism. As a result of this scholarly misreading, the image of the black preacher and the black church has been grossly misrepresented. Readers of these sermons will realize that the black church continues to be in the vanguard of social, political, and economic change within the black community, and that the black preacher, besides being the initiator of such change, has also served to nurture hope in the midst of hopelessness.

It is this hope that has enabled black Americans to survive in spite of the social evils of slavery, oppression, inhumanity, pain, brutality, racism, and persecution. Hope has enabled people to survive in the past and will enable them to survive in the future. Is the hope, however, a false hope? Is it directed primarily toward heaven? Or, is it geared to freedom and liberation in this world? The way in which these questions are answered in these sermons shows how the contributors understand the gospel and its content.

The gospel, as they see it, focuses on humanization, liberation, freedom, justice, righteousness, and the reign of God in human affairs. These qualities are promised by God; they come from God. Because they are the promises of *God,* they are *not* a false hope, but are grounded in an initiative that outruns defeat, tragedy, affliction, pain, persecution, oppression, poverty, and all social evils.

To be sure, this hope has a dual eschatological dimension to it: it is grounded both within history and beyond history. The expression "within history" has reference to a kind of realized eschatological hope. What are we working for? We are working for the actualization of the kingdom of God here on earth, the building of the promised land through the establishment of justice and righteousness as present reality. Because the kingdom will not be consummated at any one point within history, however, the expression "beyond history" becomes very important. It points to those inexhaustible possibilities in God that always remain a critique to the human predicament in any age or moment, however "advanced." These sermons show clearly that in the hope nurtured by the gospel there is an interrelationship and an interconnection between the this-worldly eschatological dimension and the otherworldly eschatological dimension.

The task of bringing together sermons from so many perspectives with a singularity of orientation was a real challenge. Therefore, I wish to thank all those who have contributed to making this exciting project a success. I am grateful to Joan Daves, executor of Martin Luther King, Jr. publications, for granting permission to reprint "The Drum Major Instinct." I am particularly appreciative of the splendid cooperation of my fellow preachers—ministers, professors, administrators, bishops, leaders from many denominations all over the country. And last but not least I want to express my profound gratitude to my secretary Eugenia Blair, and to my wife Aleta Joyce, for typing the original manuscript.

Henry J. Young

CONTENTS

THE UNIVERSITY OF ADVERSITY

WILLIAM HOLMES BORDERS

Minister of Wheat Street Baptist Church
Atlanta, Georgia

Notre Dame is a great Catholic university. Harvard is a great Eastern university. Heidelberg is a great German university. Oxford is a great English university. Columbia is a great New York university. Howard is a great capstone university. Atlanta University is a great collegiate university. The University of Adversity is a great suffering university.

The first seven of these institutions award degrees in medicine, law, business, chemistry, mathematics, and other disciplines. The University of Adversity offers degrees through suffering, misfortune, disease, slavery, and disappointment. Jews suffered for centuries under the rule of Egypt, Babylon, Persia, Assyria, and Rome. Black Americans attended the University of Adversity for 244 years; they were handcuffed, shackled, and daggered in heart.

Who does what in the University of Adversity? A quitter quits. A drunkard drinks. A drug addict takes another pill. A murderer spills blood. A weakling weakens. A blame-shifter ducks responsibility. A hypocrite double-crosses. A doubter doubts. A pessimist hides and gets lost in the darkness. But there are a few who finish, some of them cum laude, Phi Beta Kappa, and "O Lordy."

Richard Allen was snatched knee-bent from the altar in a Methodist church.

Booker T. Washington was beaten. He returned to Tuskegee. He went to chapel. One of the students said, "They have wounded our leader."

1

Robert Russa Moton had to live in continuous fear simply because he had advocated having black doctors in the Veterans Hospital at Tuskegee.

Nat Turner was executed in Southampton County, Virginia. Medgar Evers was shot in the back. Thousands of black men were lynched in the South. Monroe Work kept the record. No whites were ever brought to trial. Three civil rights workers were killed in Philadelphia, Mississippi and their bodies hidden in the sand. Four little girls were bombed to death on Sunday morning in Sunday school at Sixteenth Street Baptist Church in Birmingham, Alabama. Martin Luther King, Jr. was rifled down in Memphis, Tennessee. Clyde Manning, a black straw boss, knocked eleven blacks in the head with an ax on John Williams's farm in Jasper County. The eleven bodies were found buried in shallow graves. Clyde Manning, a black, was white John Williams's hatchet man.

Rogers Hornsby, perhaps baseball's greatest second baseman, had his best years while playing handicapped almost the entire season with a sore heel.

Tom Dempsey, a professional football player had half his foot cut off by a tractor. Kicking with a false foot, he became one of the game's best placekickers.

Burley Grimes pitched and won the deciding game in a world series as his father lay in a coffin awaiting burial.

Babe Ruth was an orphan.

Fritz Kreisler had a string of his violin break as he played before a packed audience. On his feet in perfect poise he transposed the number—played it in a different key—and continued to thrill his listeners, who didn't know until afterwards what had happened.

Bermuda grass grows faster when you try hardest to kill it.

Fox fire spreads most when you stomp it hardest.

Blindness forced Fannie Crosby to attend the University of Adversity. Shut up in darkness all her life, except for the first six weeks, she became one of the great hymn writers of Christendom, second only to Charles Wesley. Fannie Crosby finished cum laude.

Joseph, the son of Jacob finished O Lordy. Jealousy enrolled Joseph in Egyptian slavery. Instead of allowing the University of

Adversity to embitter, defeat, and break his spirit, Joseph climbed from the pit to a seat beside the throne.

Then there came a king "who knew not Joseph," and Joseph fell. You can fall. Nixon fell from the most prestigious political position on earth. Adam fell from a perfect state. Nicolas II, the last czar of Russia, was shot to death. In death he was financially rich. But what good are riches to a dead man? Though Joseph fell and suffered, his faith in freedom's future victory was never shaken. Fannie Crosby finished the University of Adversity cum laude; Joseph finished O Lordy. When God orders the freedom march, said Joseph, "Dig up my bones."

Daniel finished O Lordy, too. King Belshazzar had dumped the prophet into a den of lions. The Babylonian chief executive expected torn flesh and cracked bones. But the lions were suddenly afflicted with spiritual lockjaw. Daniel fell asleep using the shaggy manes of the lions as a pillow. My Bible tells me: "The lamb and lion shall lie down together."

Thorn-in-the-flesh Paul is my New Testament evangelist—traveling mainly by foot, writing fourteen of the New Testament's twenty-seven books. Beheaded by Nero, his spirit still lives.

John Milton was blind but he peeped into Paradise.

Helen Keller was blind and deaf. Doubly handicapped, she became one of the choice spirits of this century.

George Washington Carver was turned down by Highland because he was black. He was turned up by God because he was a genius.

Ludwig van Beethoven was deaf. He wrote music for other people's ears.

John of Arc was burned alive. The church which once condemned her later voted her a saint and built a cathedral in her honor.

Louis Pasteur had a stroke at the age of forty-six, after which he gave to the world his greatest discoveries.

John Bunyan wrote *Pilgrim's Progress,* allegory of the English language, while languishing in jail.

John Huss, reformer of the church in Bohemia, was burned to death.

3

William Tyndale was burned alive for translating the Bible into the vernacular.

Our own finest hour here at Wheat Street was when our church was burned down.

Shadrach, Meshach, and Abednego were dumped into a furnace of fire by Nebuchadnezzar.

John the Baptist lost his head to Herod.

John the seer of the Book of Revelation was banished to the Isle of Patmos.

Peter was crucified, head down.

James was killed in Jerusalem.

John Kennedy was rifled down in Dallas.

Robert Kennedy was shot to death in California.

Socrates was forced to drink poison.

Stephen was stoned to death.

The University of Adversity has a long and distinguished honor roll of graduates, people who finished cum laude, Phi Beta Kappa, and O Lordy. The list could go on and on.

Abraham Lincoln was the main human instrumentality in saving the greatest democracy of history. He was assassinated.

Mahatma Ghandi was the greatest pragmatic ethicist who ever lived; arraying soul force against military might, he freed a continent of 350 million people—and was assassinated.

Job dealt with tragic defeats, diseases, disasters, calamities, and evils. Flat on his back, hanging on by a spider's web, Job affirmed a positive faith: "The judge of all the earth must do right." He even addressed that Judge directly: "Though ye slay me, yet will I trust thee."

Moses gave the Ten Commandments while leading the world's greatest freedom march.

Jesus was the honor student above all. He graduated cum laude *and* O Lordy. Jesus mastered life. He conquered death. The rejected stone became the head of the corner. Today this unique Son of God has millions upon millions who name him "Lord and Master."

Jesus is my cum laude prophet. Jesus is my Phi Beta Kappa

master of life and conqueror of death. Jesus is my O Lordy worldwide Savior.

Jesus died on a cross.

> On a hill far away stood an old rugged cross,
> The emblem of suffering and shame;
> And I love that old cross where the dearest and best
> For a world of lost sinners was slain.

Having finished cum laude and O Lordy, Jesus enables me to go on studying—in that same university, the most famous in all the world, the one with the longest list of distinguished graduates.

WHY SIT WE HERE?

ROY C. NICHOLS

Bishop, Pittsburgh Area
Western Pennsylvania Conference
of the United Methodist Church
Pittsburgh, Pennsylvania

And there were four leprous men at the entering in of the gate: and they said one to another, Why sit we here until we die?

—2 Kings 7:3

A KINGDOM DIVIDED

Eight centuries before the birth of Christ the Jewish nation, which had been unified under King David, split in two. Jeroboam became the leader of the northern kingdom. Rehoboam, Solomon's son and successor, held dominion over the southern kingdom.

Both of these separate kingdoms were subsequently defeated and the people carried off into captivity by outside enemies. The reference in the text describes an incident during the period when the Syrians, under General Benhadad, swept down upon the northern kingdom and laid siege to Samaria, the capitol city.

Siege was the ultimate strategy in ancient warfare. If a city could not be conquered by the sheer power of armed force, because of the strength of its walls, the enemy would simply encamp, surrounding the city, cutting off all of its supplies and wait until the inhabitants were starved into a forced surrender.

Samaria was in great distress. Her people were devastated by hunger. In fact, conditions were so desperate that some of the Samarians were eating the flesh of their own children.

THE LEPROUS PLIGHT

Suddenly, the author of the Second Book of Kings shifts the scene. Quarantined outside the city walls are four starving leprous men, considering their options. Lepers, as you know, were kept in complete isolation in ancient times. The knowledge of the contagion of their dreadful disease forced upon them rigidly restricted isolation.

So, these separated brethren were considering their fate. If they should attempt to crash the gate of the city, they might be stoned to death. But even if they succeeded in entering, there was no food. Thus they would die. If they decided to move toward the Syrian encampment, just beyond the ridge of the nearby hills, where food was plentiful, they would doubtless be killed on sight; not only because they were lepers, but because they were the enemy. The third option was simply to remain where they were and die without complications. It was out of this deep distress, that one of the leprous men spoke to the others saying: "Why sit we here until we die?"

DECISIONS, DECISIONS

Decision-making is a difficult business, especially when every choice involves a perilous risk. But there is an even greater danger in just waiting for the worst to happen!

They tell a story of a sailor in boot training whose company was taken to a high platform, forty feet above a pool of water. Each man was instructed to jump. But one fellow just stood at the top of the diving board and refused to move. He was scared. "Jump!" shouted his commanding officer. But there was no response. Finally, the officer screamed, "What would you do if you were on the high seas and your ship was shot out from under you?" The sailor frantically responded, "I'd let the board sink another thirty-five feet and then jump!" Little did he realize if he waited that long, the suction from the sinking vessel would pull him under.

Not very long ago I heard an interesting definition of a bachelor. Now, I must make it clear I have no bias against bachelors, but a good anecdote is worth repeating. "A bachelor is a man who has failed to embrace his opportunities." There are some lessons in this text which may be opportunities. There are some lessons in this text which may be appropriately applied to the individual, to the church, and to black Americans.

POWER TO BECOME

Christianity begins with the crisis of sin in the life of the individual. The whole tenor of the gospel is to free us from the power and the penalty of sin and to make possible what Jesus called "the abundant life."

You remember the instance when Jesus met the man who was languishing on his cot, crippled and unable to move. The Master said to him: "Rise, take up thy bed, and walk." Jesus had a profound understanding of a kind of illness which can be more restrictive than the physical ailments. And so he challenged the crippled man to use his own strength first; the rest of the cure was accomplished by the miraculous empowerment of God.

Sin and self-pity are the most insidious of all human illnesses. They keep us pondering at a point of indecision. But to gain release, each individual must reach out and seize the blessing. Clothed with the capability of a new life we are able to do all things through Christ who strengthens us.

Some time ago the Carnegie Foundation made a study of the plight of the small colleges in America. Among its conclusions was the observation that many of these struggling educational enterprises were suffering from the "trauma of self-doubt." One of the great phrases of the Apostle Paul was "I can do all things through Christ who strengtheneth me." If you can shake off the tethering impediment of sin and doubt, there is no circumstance that can keep you down, no adversary that can permanently conquer your spirit, no odds which you cannot overcome.

A MESSAGE FOR THE CHURCHES

This text also has something to say to the churches. As ecumenical enthusiasm subsides, one hears the growing tones of theological controversy emerging.

Fundamentalists, for one thing, are saying that organized Christendom has forsaken the authority of the Bible. While their admonishing word is timely, we must remember that Jesus had his greatest difficulty with the literalistic dogmatism of the Pharisees. They insisted upon the letter of the law and ignored its spirit and intent. In a doctrinal statement set forth by the United Methodist Church at its 1972 General Conference, it was stated that the guidelines for Christian interpretation are based upon Scriptures, tradition, experience, and reason. All of these are necessary to rightly divide the word of truth.

Secondly, there are certain charismatics who keep suggesting a divisive gradation of spiritual gifts. Surely we need the enthusiasm of the manifest power of the Holy Spirit; but Paul made it explicitly clear that the same Spirit gives to all a diversity of gifts, that love is the supreme ingredient, and that no spiritual gift is superior to another. We differ in our points of excellence, but our unity is in Christ!

Finally, liberal activists sometimes insist that deeds of righteousness are the only genuine manifestation of Christian credibility. Their testimony is timely. But it is to be remembered that the primary attention of the religious quest centers around our thirst for God. The cultivation of the inner sensitivity of the soul to the presence and power of the Almighty is as important as giving a cup of cold water to the thirsty and rescuing the weak from the ordeal of oppression.

The church needs the fullness of the gospel in all its aspects— the word, the charisma, and the action. But controversy among the "saints" dissipates the energy which strident decision-making requires. Christians need to take the offensive! Every local church must be Christ's fellowship of persons engaged in faith, witness, and service.

THE BLACK EXPERIENCE

This text also has something to say to the black brothers and sisters in America, who have already waited too long for freedom to be given. In the context of human oppression freedom never comes as a gift. It is achieved through excellence, persistence, and unswerving determination.

Black America has lost the best endowment of too many of its great minds in endless concentration upon the racial struggle per se. True, the days of confrontation are not past, but if black Americans are ever to achieve true equality then doctors, craftsmen, scientists, mothers, fathers, dentists, sanitation workers, preachers, teachers, and the whole plethora of vocations must be studded with the sparkling genius of exceptional black contribution.

Now I'm not naive enough to believe that the sheer weight of skills and personal excellence will totally win the struggle against racism. For racism is a manifestation of the inclination of the strong to take advantage of the weak. And black Americans with power tend to succumb to the same temptation.

Black comedians and movie producers are involved in seducing the better talents of the black community for monetary gain. To glorify the "Superfly" image of the pimp, the prostitute, the clown, the dope pusher, and the charlatan is to implant the seeds of regression in the limited black experience. These negative image makers must be discouraged by our refusing to patronize their degrading performances. In their place, new visual media must project the image of hard work, sterling character, and the perfection of those indispensable skills which alone can purchase a better future. "Sounder" was an excellent step in the right direction.

THE LEPERS REVISITED

The four lepers, engrossed in the throes of deep decision, prodded by the searching question Why sit we here? were finally pushed into action. They decided that they would march directly into the armed camp of the Syrians. At least there was the prospect of food, in spite of the risk of death. So they arose at sunset with their heads erect, and walking side by side they mounted the crest of the hill. The setting sun cast their long shadows on the ground, the silhouette of their bodies against the horizon making them look like four massive giants.

When the Syrians saw them approaching, with such resolute determination, they thought they heard the noise of chariots, the pounding of hoofs of an army of horses, and the clashing of many sabers. Supposing these four men to be the vanguard of a great liberating army, the Syrian forces turned in panic and fled, leaving their tents, their armor, their horses and chariots, and their food. So by this singular act of courage on the part of the four leprous men—outcasts—that day Israel was saved.

WE SHALL OVERCOME

The late Dr. Martin Luther King told a story of the early days of the bus boycott in Montgomery, Alabama. Before Montgomery's black citizens began to walk rather than suffer the indignities of riding segregated buses, it was common to see clusters of black young people and old-timers standing on the corner grinning and swapping jokes, scratching their heads, playing checkers. But when they discovered a new sense of purpose as the deep meanings of "We Shall Overcome" possessed them, the street-corner scene changed. Clusters of black Alabamians could still be seen, but now they were talking in low tones, backs straight, with an evident new sense of dignity.

They had found in Brother Martin the resilience and the courage to move. It required personal sacrifice, discipline, and organized effort. But when they mounted the crest of the hill to face the opposing army, there in the streets of Montgomery their splendid decorum and unyielding manner caused the enemy of discrimination and prejudice to flee.

Why sit we here? . . .

THE SPIRIT OF CHRIST AT WORK IN HUMAN RELATIONS

HERBERT BELL SHAW

Presiding Bishop, First Episcopal Area
of the African Methodist Episcopal Zion Church
Wilmington, North Carolina

> The spirit of the Lord is upon me; because the Lord hath anointed me to preach good tidings to the poor; he hath sent me to proclaim release to the captives, the opening of the eyes of the blind, and setting at liberty of them that are bruised, and the proclaiming of God's year of jubilee.
> —Isaiah 61:1–2; Luke 4:18–19

Here we have the very essence of the things needed by a world that is lost in its search for the "abundant life." The social implication of these words, which Jesus lifted up from the dust of antiquity and made the clarion campaign issue of his life, is both imminent and supreme.

Jesus knew "man" and he knew "society." The abundant life, spiritual and temporal, is an undeniable priority. No man or group of men possesses the right to act in any way that would mitigate against total access to the good life.

The Psalmist declares: "The earth is the Lord's and the fulness thereof; . . . and they that dwell therein." Here the "Earth" and the "dwellers" are tied together in one package and no social system has the right to separate one from the other.

Jesus found that the social and political system of his day, the "establishment" if you please, was stacked against the free flow of the blessings of life to all who were by divine nature heirs and joint heirs. Jesus offered as proof of his divine ministry the following facts:

First, he had received his appointment from the great I Am, and it was to preach good tidings to the poor.

Second, he was commissioned and sent to proclaim release to the captives.

Third, he was ordered to open the eyes of the blind.

Fourth, he was commanded to set at liberty them that were bruised.

Fifth, he was deputized to proclaim God's year of jubilee.

This programmatic mandate seems to determine the lines upon which the redemptive energies of the kingdom of God should work in human relations. This five-point program is designed to meet a fivefold need.

First, there is to be good news for the poor. "The poor" are the economically disinherited. We must not make the mistake of stretching the connotation of *poor* to mean the spiritually disinherited, though it is true that where spiritual poverty abounds, economic poverty is systematically imposed and sanctioned—to the detriment of those who are the victims of the establishment.

Christianity must be concerned with poverty. We cannot escape involvement in this area. If we do, we are not followers of our Lord, who aches with the hunger of the hungry: "I was hungry and ye fed me."

What does it mean to bring good news to the economically disinherited? Put them on the welfare rolls? Give them charity? Welfare is good, but not good enough. The poor do not need charity; they need justice.

To preach contentment with the status quo is not to preach good news. The poor should not be content with poverty, for poverty is not the will of God. His will is that we have life and have it in abundance. The earth is ready to supply all our needs bountifully. Poverty is the result of man's exploitation of his fellowman in the pursuit of greed. Poverty could be eradicated today if we had the collective will to do so.

Second, the captives must be set free. Here we are talking about the politically and socially disinherited. Christianity must maintain its dedication to freedom, total liberation. We must not be satisfied until equality of opportunity is enjoyed by everyone. We must not rest until this blessing of Christ is common to all. We must build together a society in which every child born into that society will have equal privilege with every other child who is a part of that society—equal opportunity to food and shelter, an adequate education, the respect of his contemporaries, gainful employment, and social security without any discrimination whatsoever.

Third, the eyes of the blind must be opened. Christianity has a dual message. Its good news must be liberation for both body and soul. We must declare our concern for the physically disinherited. Sickness is not the will of God, but an enemy to be conquered. It was for this reason that the Lord of life healed the sick and raised the dead.

Fourth, there is to be a setting at liberty of them that are bruised. Here we are called upon to give the gospel of hope to the morally and spiritually disinherited. Jesus said, "I am come to strengthen with forgiveness them that are bruised." Christianity has a beautiful message for those who are inwardly bruised by sin, guilt, and fear. It sends out a shining ray of light to those that are lost and groping on paths where for centuries some have become wounded as others transgress the moral laws of nature and society. It heralds the good news of regeneration, reconciliation, and restoration. It reminds us all that every saint has a past and every sinner a future. We must always remember that we do not break God's law; the law remains inexorably the same—we break only ourselves as we violate it.

Fifth, we are to proclaim the year of the Lord's jubilee. The reference is to the Old Testament practice whereby every fifty years there was a year of jubilee in which all debts were declared settled, all lands redistributed, all slaves freed, and all nations allowed to start out anew on the basis of a closer bond of equality and brotherhood. Jesus proclaimed this expunging of the past and a fresh beginning as his program. He universalized it and brought it into its true perspective. He pointed out the need for collective regeneration in order that a new order might be born. In this new dimension of the Lord's jubilee we work from the individual out to the social order and from the social order back to the individual; work must be done in *both* directions.

Here is a fivefold prescription which is fully adequate to heal the ills of a sick and dying social order. Written by an ancient prophet, refilled and recommended by Jesus who knew its powers at firsthand, it is a medicine that can heal us—individually and collectively—so that we might live buoyantly and abundantly in our time.

THE POLITICAL AND SOCIAL
IMPLICATIONS OF THE MINISTRY

ANDREW YOUNG

*Congressman from the Fifth District
Atlanta, Georgia*

I want to begin my discussion of the political and social implications of the ministry by focusing on a previous pastorate in south-
west Georgia in a little town called Thomasville. I went to
Thomasville upon graduation from the Hartford Seminary Foundation. At that time, about twenty years ago, I firmly believed that
it pleased God by the foolishness of preaching to save men's
souls. My ministry was successful in terms of the way success in
ministry was normally evaluated in those days: attendance was
increasing, the financial status of the congregation was strong,
and the church was rendering outstanding services to the community.

But I discovered that there was something lacking in my ministry. Although there was much spiritualization going on within
the church, and the social programs were effective in terms of
ministering to various needs of the people, there was a basic need
that we were not meeting. We were not meeting this need because the black people of Thomasville had a very pessimistic view
of the present and future of that community. Every weekend one
of my members would get into trouble with the white establishment. My members wanted to do what was right, but they con-
stantly found themselves dragged down by the society in which
they lived.

The educational level of many blacks was superior to that of
many whites in the community, but the structure of Thomasville

systematically caused blacks to work side by side with the whites, doing the very same jobs, while receiving wages that were far inferior to those of the whites. And not only that: many of those same blacks, after working on a job for fifteen or twenty years, would have whites with less education and only six months training appointed as their supervisors. Obviously, this created intense frustrations among the blacks, and at this point I began to ask myself, what does it take to change society? I then concluded that it was going to take more than preaching.

I realized that I could preach to my people until I became exhausted, my members could shout until they were good and happy, but that wasn't going to affect the life they lived when they left church and went outside into that hostile community and society. Once the people left the Sunday services they were not treated as "God's children." They were referred to rather as "boy," "nigger," "captain," or some other degrading name. I then began to realize that the ministry, if it was going to change social, economic, and educational conditions, had to have a political dimension to it. I understood that a voteless people is a hopeless people. And, I understood that by becoming politically oriented, the church can assist in bringing about the changes in society that will break down the walls of oppression, enslavement, racism, segregation, unequal employment, and other social evils. I became awakened to the realization that the ministry had to have social and political implications. It is not enough to minister to the spiritual well-being of a people; we must also transform the structures of society that prevent people from relating to each other as authentic persons.

I also learned from this community that the ministry has a cost to it—there is a cross that we as ministers must be willing to bear. Can we be Christians without having a cross? The hymnologist answered this question when he said,

> Must Jesus bear the cross alone,
> And all the world go free?
> No, there's a cross for everyone,
> And there's a cross for me.

Those of us who participated in the Civil Rights movement with the late Martin Luther King, Jr. realized that we had a cross to bear. When Dr. King invited a hundred preachers to come together and form the Southern Christian Leadership Conference, he was looking for persons who realized the socio-political dimensions of the ministry; each minister had to be willing to bear his own cross.

If the ministers would unite and embrace their ministry within the scope of the social, economic, spiritual, educational, and political dimensions of society, we would be able to reconcile man both with God and with his brother. This approach will break down the polarization between blacks and whites. This is what it takes to have a relevant ministry. We must be able to change the situation in which people live, as well as change the people themselves. The problems of people are interconnected with every aspect of society. Therefore, if the church can have a ministry that concerns itself with the totality of society, we can begin to change the lives of people.

Black Americans have definitely made some significant strides politically, and the black church has been the vanguard of this political activism. We now have the right to vote, to eat at lunch counters, and to be treated as human beings. Yet black Americans still find themselves in disproportionate numbers among the unemployed, the dispossessed, and the poor. It is still true that a high school graduate who is white can earn more than a black college graduate. Therefore, we still have a problem of economic injustice to deal with. We must transform the political system so that economic changes can come about. We must create the kind of political climate in which economic justice will flow down like waters from the political system.

This is the kind of ministry that it is going to take to feed the hungry, clothe the naked, open the eyes of those who are blind, and heal those who are sick. To feed the hungry today might mean to have congressmen who will support the food stamps program, and clothing the naked might mean to increase the minimum wage. Issues such as these are not only social, economic, and political—they are religious!

Black Americans used to sing the spiritual, "I got shoes, you got shoes, all God's children got shoes;/ When I get to heaven gonna put on my shoes . . ." But that is not the way I pray any longer. Today I say, "Thy kingdom come, thy will be done here on earth, even as it is in heaven. Give us this day our daily bread." We want bread today, not when we get to heaven; we want shoes now, not when we get to heaven.

All these concerns are a part of the ministry. In order to accomplish them we must embrace the social, economic, educational, and political dimensions of life within the framework of our ministry. This is the kind of total ministry that made Martin Luther King, Jr. such an outstanding figure in our generation. And, where did he learn of it?

WHAT DOES IT MEAN TO BE SAVED?

JAMES H. CONE

Professor of Systematic Theology
Union Theological Seminary
New York, New York

Unfortunately, the concept of salvation has been greatly distorted in the history of Christian thought. This has been due partly to the inordinate influence of Greek philosophy on Christian language and partly to the political status of the church since Constantine. The former, Greek philosophy, separated salvation from history; and the latter, political favoritism, produced a view of the gospel that was unrelated to the interests of the oppressed.

Greek philosophy, for example, was influential in the early debates on Christology. The driving force of Athanasius's advocacy of the *homoousia* doctrine was his concern for the motif of salvation, the doctrine of redemption. He contended that one cannot say that *God* redeems humanity unless the Savior, Jesus Christ, is of the "same substance" with the Father. I think Athanasius came out on the right side of the argument, but for the wrong reasons. In his view, salvation is identical with divinization; that is, God became human in order that humanity might become divine. Thus, salvation is removed from history.

The tendency to separate salvation from history played into the hands of the wielders of political power. If salvation involves divinization or spiritualization, it is no longer necessary to view Christianity as a religion of revolution against the powers of injustice. It becomes easy to think of slave masters and oppressors as Christians. For after all, the only thing that matters is the *spiritual* condition of people, not their civil status.

Throughout the history of Christian thought false distinctions have been made between the spiritual and the physical, as if political freedom is either unrelated or secondary to God's work of salvation in Jesus Christ. Whenever theology defines the gospel independently of liberation (i.e., independently of social, economic, and political freedom), it is planting the seed that separates spiritual freedom from physical freedom. Unfortunately, Euro-American theology is famous for making the distinction between the physical and the spiritual; and despite the physical oppression of people on the basis of that distinction, contemporary theologians still contend, with Hans Küng, that "the purely religious character of the reign of God is not in dispute."

In order to unmask the radical error of that view of salvation, it is necessary to return to the Scripture and see how salvation is there defined. In the Old Testament, salvation is grounded in history and is identical with that righteousness of God which delivers people from bondage. Literally, the root meaning of the word *salvation* is "to be wide or spacious, to develop without hindrance, and thus, ultimately, to have victory in battle." The Savior is the one who has power to gain victory, and the saved are the oppressed who have been set free. For Israel, it is Yahweh who is the Savior because "the Lord *saved* Israel that day from the hand of the Egyptians; and Israel saw the Egyptians dead upon the seashore" (Exod. 14:30). That is why the people sang:

> I will sing to the Lord, for he has triumphed gloriously;
>   the horse and his rider he has thrown into the sea.
> The Lord is my strength and my song,
>   and he has become my salvation;
> this is my God, and I will praise him, . . .
> The Lord is a man of war;
>   the Lord is his name.
>
> (Exod. 15:1–3)

Here salvation is God's deliverance of the people from political danger. It is his divine righteousness to liberate the weak and the oppressed. Salvation therefore is an historical event of rescue, a bestowal of freedom.

There are a number of terms which describe God's saving activity: deliverance, redemption, healing. Almost without exception, in the Old Testament the deliverer, redeemer, and healer is

God, and the delivered, the redeemed, and the healed are oppressed people. It is impossible to understand the Old Testament
view of salvation without recognizing that salvation means God's
deliverance of helpless victims from physical suffering or political
menace.

In the New Testament, the Old Testament emphasis on God as
the One who effects salvation, and on salvation as historical liberation, is not denied but reinforced and carried through to its most
radical consequences. In the New Testament as in the Old, God
is the Savior par excellence, and his salvation is the revolutionary
historical liberation of the oppressed of the land. That is why it is
reported that Jesus was born in a stable at Bethlehem, and why
Mary describes the divine meaning of his coming presence with
these words.

> My soul magnifies the Lord,
> and my spirit rejoices in God my Savior,
>
> . . . .
>
> He has shown strength with his arm,
> he has scattered the proud in the imagination of their hearts,
> he has put down the mighty from their thrones,
> and exalted those of low degree;
> he has filled the hungry with good things,
> and the rich he has sent empty away.
>
> (Luke 1:46–47, 51–53)

The identification of salvation with freedom from bondage in
history is revealed in the New Testament through Jesus' identity
with the poor. He came to and for the poor; he ate with the outcasts, the "bad characters" of his day, the ones whom the Pharisees called "sinners." He healed the sick, gave sight to the blind,
and restored health to the lame and the crippled. When John sent
his disciples to Jesus asking, "Are you he who is to come, or
shall we look for another?" Jesus replied: "Go and tell John what
you have seen and heard: the blind receive their sight, the lame
walk, lepers are cleansed, and the deaf hear, the dead are raised
up, the poor have good news preached to them" (Luke 7:20f).
These acts locate salvation in history, in the concreteness of
human existence. If the kingdom of God (God's rule) is identical
with Jesus' person, and if his person is inseparable from his
work, then there is little doubt as to what salvation means: it is

the bringing of wholeness and health in the conditions of brokenness, the bringing of peace and justice where oppression exists. In a word, it is the restoration of people to their true humanity. Salvation is the bestowal of freedom for the unfree, redemption for the slave, acquittal for the convicted, and deliverance for the captives.

I suggested earlier that the New Testament accepts the historicity of the Old Testament view of salvation and carries it through to radical conclusions. The radicalness of the New Testament view lies not in its rejection of the historical character of salvation. To reject the historical aspect of salvation leads to passivity; it makes religion the opiate of the people. The New Testament, while accepting history, does not limit salvation to history. As long as people are bound to history, they are bound to law, and hence to death. If death is the ultimate power and life has no future beyond this world, then the rulers of the state who control the military are in the place of God. They have the future in their hands, and the oppressed can be made to obey the law of injustice. But if the oppressed, while living in history, can see beyond it, if they can visualize an eschatological future beyond this world, then the "sigh of oppressed creature," to use Marx's phrase, can become a revolutionary cry of rebellion against the established order. It is this revolutionary cry that is granted in the Resurrection of Jesus.

Salvation then, in the New Testament view, is not simply freedom in history; it is freedom to affirm that future which is *beyond* history. Indeed, because we know that death has been conquered, we are truly free to be human *in* history, knowing that we have a "home over yonder." "The home over yonder," vividly and artistically described in the slave songs, is the gift of salvation granted in the Resurrection of Jesus.

If this "otherness" in salvation is not taken with utmost seriousness, then there is no way to be sustained now in the struggle against present injustice. The oppressed will get tired. They will fear the risks of freedom. They will say as the Israelites said to Moses when they found themselves trapped between Pharaoh's army and the Red Sea: "Is it because there are no graves in Egypt that you have taken us away to die in the wilderness? What have you done to us, in bringing us out of Egypt?" (Exod. 14:11). The fear of freedom and the risks contained in struggle are an ever present reality. But the "otherness" of salvation, its transcendence beyond history, introduces a *factor* that makes a difference. The *difference* is not that we are taken *out* of history while living on earth—that would be an opium. Rather our being is planted firmly *in* history because we know that death is not the goal of history.

The transcendence-factor in salvation helps us to realize that our fight for justice is God's fight too; and his presence in Jesus' Resurrection has already defined what the ultimate outcome will be. It was this knowledge that enabled black slaves to live in history but not to be defeated by their limitations in history. To be sure, they sang about the fear of "sinking down" and the dread of being a "motherless child." They encountered trouble and the agony of being alone where "I couldn't hear nobody pray." They encountered death and expressed it in song:

> Soon one mornin' death comes a creepin' in my room.
> O my Lawd, O my Lawd, what shall I do?

Death was a terrible reality for black slaves, and it visited the slave quarters leaving orphans behind.

> Death done been here, took my mother an' gone.
> O my Lawd, what shall I do?
> Death done been here, left me a motherless child,
> O my Lawd, what shall I do?

In these songs are expressed the harsh realities of history and the deep sense of dread at the very thought of death. But because the slaves knew or believed that death had been conquered in Jesus' Resurrection, they could also transcend death and interpret salvation as a heavenly, eschatological reality. That is why they also sang:

> You needn't mind my dying,
> Jesus' goin' to make up my dying bed.
> In my room I know,
> Somebody is going to cry,
> All I ask you to do for me,
> Just close my dying eyes.

24

TRANSFORMING THE LAND OF OPPRESSION INTO THE PROMISED LAND

CHARLES B. COPHER

Vice President for Academic Affairs
Interdenominational Theological Center
Atlanta, Georgia

The Old Testament books Genesis through Joshua present the basic structure of one of the world's most interesting and significant stories. It is the story of the "promised land." Briefly stated, the story is that the God of the patriarchs Abraham, Isaac, and Jacob promised the country of Canaan to Abraham and his descendants forever. After an extended stay as slaves in Egypt these descendants were led out of slavery by Moses; they were led to the borders of the land promised to their fathers. And under Joshua, so one version of the story goes, occupation and possession of the land was accomplished.

Much of what is in the remaining books of the Old Testament, and even in the New Testament, is commentary on the theme of the promised land. And in many respects the story of the promised land has been the story of those whom today we might call Zionist Jews.

But the story of the promised land has not been solely the story of Jews. It became the story of others who have adopted and adapted it to themselves as some kind of new Israel. Thus the early white settlers of New England and of other parts of North America regarded the new country as their promised land, they even gave their new towns biblical place names such as Bethlehem and New Canaan. The founding fathers of the United States of America also regarded the land as their land of promise; they rebelled against King George as against an Egyptian Pharaoh.

And unto this day immigrants have continued to view America as the promised land.

The promised land, however, has been more than an image of hope for Jews, both ancient and modern, and more than a national dream for most white Americans. It became and has remained for two hundred years a theme in the life of Afro-Americans. And this, despite the fact that black Americans did not flee to America's shores from an Egyptian oppression—they came in chains— and what for the white man was the promised land was and to varying degrees has remained for the black man a land of oppression, so that the black man viewing white oppression as Egyptian slavery came to sing:: "Go down, Moses, 'way down in Egypt's land./ Tell ole Pharaoh, Let my people go!" At least by the time of the Revolutionary War, when many blacks fought side by side with white colonists against the British Pharaoh, Afro-Americans took over this prominent biblical theme in relation to America. They entertained a hope that the land of oppression might become for them also the land of promise.

The history of the black man in America from that time until the present is the history of a people held in tension between two poles: between America (or some part of it) regarded as Canaan, and some place *other* than America as the yearned-for land of promise. Well-marked periods may be observed in Afro-American history when this tension between the two poles has been most acute: the Revolutionary War period; the period 1815–1865; the period of Reconstruction and its aftermath, 1875–1900; and the period 1960 to the present. It was in the midst of this last tumultuous period that Martin Luther King, Jr. could proclaim that he had "been to the mountaintop" and "seen the promised land."

During these periods, over against America (or some part of it) other parts of the earth have been looked to as the promised land: Haiti, Canada, but most often and most consistently Africa. For Martin Delany, MacNeal Turner, Marcus Garvey, others before and after them, the land has been Africa; a few blacks in recent years have even been to Africa in order to "spy out the land." But concurrently there have been the Frederick Douglasses, Booker T. Washingtons, and Martin Luther Kings who have maintained that

America, at least in prospect, is the land of promise. All these latter have agreed with Frank Wellington Gage that for Afro-Americans the United States is not Egypt and Africa is not Canaan.

Indeed, neither Africa nor any other place abroad can be or ought to be the promised land for black Americans. At least in potential, America must be that land—for the black man as also for others. It must become that for all or it will be that for none.

At this point in American history God is calling the Afro-American with, in, and through him to transform the land of oppression into the promised land. Toward that end God is calling Afro-Americans to engage in three immediate tasks: (1) to place the church once again at the center of black community life, and (2) to recapture the faith of the fathers, and (3) to evangelize.

THE CHURCH AT THE CENTER

Figures vary with respect to the percentage of Afro-Americans who at any given time were adherents to the Christian faith, and members of the church. Yet one thing is certain in Afro-American history: until fairly recent times, the vast majority of blacks were directly influenced by the black Christian church. Indeed, the black Christian church has been at the very core of black community life. It has been the religious, social, political, economic—you name it—institution par excellence. Thus, in 1903, W. E. B. Du Bois could write, "The Negro church of today is the social center of Negro life in the United States, and the most characteristic expression of African character . . ., the church often stands as a real conserver of morals, a strengthener of family life, and the final authority on what is good and right."

That was in 1903. What about today? Times are different. E. U. Essien-Udom wrote in 1962 that "the Negro church remains an important institution in Negro life." And even more recently young blacks who had written off the black church are coming again to see it as a viable institution. They are beginning to realize that the black church is still and in many instances the only institution with promise of being the vehicle for black liberation.

It is for us who are church people, though, to realize something that goes beyond what recent deprecators of the church are able

27

to grasp. It is for us to know that judgment does begin within the house of God—in more ways than one. Our times demand that we see the church, the living body of Christ, in potentially new and liberating roles, that we enlarge our concept of the ministries the church can and must perform—seeking and saving the lost, providing abundant life for shepherdless sheep, and saving the world rather than condemning it. God's mandate is upon us, and if we fail there is no other plan. Hence the necessity of restoring the church to the place in the black community that it once held. And not for the sake of the church itself, but rather for the ministries it must perform. Those who are committed to the church must rally to the call expressed in the familiar hymn:

> Rise up, O people of God!
> The Church for you doth wait,
> Her strength unequal to the task;
> Rise up and make her great!

THE FAITH OF THE FATHERS

For a decade or more it was popular for numerous blacks to disparage and ridicule not only the church but also the faith of the fathers. They adversely criticized the strategies employed for survival—except those of the militant and violence-preaching fathers. For critics, only the Gabriel Prossers, the Denmark Veseys, and the Nat Turners deserve a place in the black hall of fame. Yet in that hall of fame belong also those who preached liberation apart from violence, those who gave first emphasis to survival. Survival has always been a prerequisite for liberation: a dead man is incapable of struggling for liberation.

And know this, it was the *faith* of the fathers that enabled them to survive as well as to die—their faith in a loving God who is a God of justice, love, and mercy, a God of providence. One cannot read the writing of such fathers as Richard Allen, David Walker, Frederick Douglass, and Nathaniel Paul without noting their use of the Scriptures, especially the writings of the great prophets, that emphasize justice, love, mercy, and providence.

Again, during the decade now passing, some of us have forsaken the exodus theme of our history in favor of an exile theme. We have declared, often not knowing what we meant, our inability to "sing the Lord's song in a strange land." By contrast the fathers and their spiritual descendants, because of their faith, were and are able to sing of God's providence even in a land of oppression—not only in a Babylonian exile but also in an Egyptian enslavement. Throughout our history those possessed of the fathers' faith have been able, however horrible the circumstances, to sing:

> God of our weary years,
> God of our silent tears,
> Thou who hast brought us thus far on the way;
> Thou who hast by Thy might
> Led us into the light,
> Keep us forever in the path, we pray.
> Lest our feet stray from the places, Our God, where we met Thee,
> Lest, our hearts drunk with the wine of the world, we forget Thee;
> Shadowed beneath Thy hand,
> May we forever stand,
> True to our God, true to our native land.

Even those who disclaim the faith of the fathers join in singing that "anthem." Those of us who claim the faith have continued to sing it across the years, and to add: "We've come this far by faith, leaning on the Lord." And it is for all of us as a people to recapture for our salvation, our liberation, the faith that enabled the fathers to survive and make strides toward freedom.

PREACHING THE GOSPEL

We have affirmed the need to transform the land of oppression into the promised land, and we have looked at two immediate tasks to which we are called in that connection. The reality of plain human nature, however, does not permit us to stop where we are—not yet. For it forces us again to raise the question Is that all? Even if we did everything called for, if we placed the church once again at the center of life in the black community and if we recaptured the faith of the fathers, would we then experience the promised land in all its fullness?

Some even of our black theologians have been saying, "Yes, indeed, and away with all otherworldly trivia!" Human nature being what it is, however, even the best of us inevitably pollute the pure atmosphere of every land of promise. Because we are human those of us who yesterday were the oppressed become today's oppressors. Thus shall oppression ever be with us—and the need for an ultimate forgiveness and liberation.

The only adequate answer must take into consideration the fact that even the biblical story of the promised land does not end in the Old Testament. The New Testament writer of the Book of Hebrews adds a concluding note. Even Abraham, to whom the promise was first made, found on earth no abiding city. Consequently he looked for a city whose builder and maker is God. No matter how ideal or fair earth may become, there is still that which forces us to spiritualize when we sing:

> On Jordan's stormy banks I stand,
> And cast a wishful eye
> To Canaan's fair and happy land,
> Where my possessions lie.
> I am bound for the promised land, . . .

THE KINGDOM OF GOD

A. ROGER WILLIAMS

*Minister of Union Baptist Church
Hartford, Connecticut*

Thy kingdom come.

—Matthew 6:10

Jesus' preaching, as that of John the Baptist, began with the concept of the kingdom of God. Someone reading Matthew's Gospel might wonder at the phrase "kingdom of *heaven*" appearing so often.

William Barclay explains in his readable book, *The Mind of Jesus:* "The reason for the two forms is this. The name of God was so holy that no devout Jew would lightly take it on his lips. One of the simplest ways to avoid the use of the name of God was to speak of heaven instead. Matthew is the most Jewish of all the Gospel writers. He therefore, instead of speaking about the kingdom of God, habitually speaks about the kingdom of heaven."

What does Jesus mean by the expression "kingdom of God?" Any careful study of the Master's kingdom sayings and kingdom parables leads one to conclude it was the sovereignty of God, the rule of God. A. W. Argyle in his *God In The New Testament* writes, "The primary and principal meaning in the phrase 'the kingdom of God' is the kingly rule, the sovereignty, the reign of God's holy healing, saving love, and wisdom." Jesus sums it up in the prayer which includes the petition: "Thy kingdom come, Thy will be done on earth, as it is in heaven." Millions daily offer this prayer. The areas in which we can pray for and seek to actualize the needed reality are legion. I would mention a few of them:

31

RACE RELATIONS

The scholarly Du Bois prophesied back in 1903 that color would be *the* problem of the twentieth century. It has been and is. Not as blatant and open as it was in the days when lynchings were publicly advertised and victims were mutilated by the raging mob as they hanged or burned. But racism is alive and kicking throughout the land. In politics, let a Tom Bradley run for mayor and his supposedly civil opponent, himself a mayor, substitutes an emotional racist appeal for facts. In industry, how many trained black electricians, plumbers, carpenters, and bricklayers are allowed to join the skilled trades unions? In so-called liberal Boston, would there have been such a hassle over busing had there been quality education in the ghetto schools? Blacks are more concerned with what they get than where they go to get it. In church, how often do whites flee to the suburbs rather than minister to blacks and other minorities? Yet are not these "the least" of whom Christ speaks, whom he calls "my brethren"?

Can we pray "Thy kingdom come" oblivious to the fact that God is not concerned with pigmentation of skin half so much as with having "a humble and contrite heart"? Our prayer is that the kingdom of God may come in the area of race relations.

SOCIETAL CONCERNS

The parable of the last judgment makes abundantly clear Christ's concern for the disinherited and oppressed. He identifies with them. He who feeds the hungry feeds him. He who clothes the naked clothes him. He who visits the prisoners visits him. "Inasmuch as ye have done it unto one of the least of these my brethren, ye have done it unto me."

It is true that if religion begins with the individual it begins, but if it ends with the individual it ends. Too much religion is totally individualistic. God save us from wanting the kingdom in our hearts to the exclusion of all concern about the youth who tells us that heroin is his shepherd. God save us from feasting abundantly every day while the Lazaruses of Asia, Africa, and urban America sit at our palatial gates awaiting the crumbs from Dives's table. God save us from indifference to the indigent youth who spends months in jail awaiting a trial because he has no bail money. Recently a militant, Lee Otis Johnson, was given a thirty-five year sentence in a Texas court because he sold a marijuana cigarette. In another court in the same state a judge's son was tried for the same thing. Did he serve time? No! He was given two years probation. Is that equal justice?

John Ruskin challenges us. He puts it bluntly, "If you do not wish God's kingdom, don't pray for it. But if you do, you must do more than pray for it; you must work for it." God's kingdom calls for effort, sensitive and massive efforts, in the affairs of society.

THE WORLD OF THE NATIONS

Speaking at the Greater Hartford Community College some years ago, Dr. Benjamin E. Mays outlined three contemporary social evils: racism, hunger, and war. No nation wins a war today. Both sides lose. The land is scarred. Famine and disease ensue. Money that could go for a hundred creative purposes is channeled to purposes of demolition and destruction that prove nothing in a world such as ours. Someone has wisely offered the truth that "men will carry guns until they learn to carry the cross."

Martin Luther King, Jr., saw what the Vietnam fiasco was doing. So did we. He saw money diverted from human needs and used to destroy a land and people many thousands of miles away. He saw black youth drafted in disproportionate numbers. He knew what the malevolent smile of the military-industrial complex meant. So he spoke, and he acted. Expecting to be misunderstood by friend and foe, he nonetheless incarnated his convictions. Though his cause would suffer, his conscience would not.

When will the church take seriously Sir Douglas Haig's dictum, "It is the business of the church to make my business impossible"? When will we implement the words of the ancient prophet:

> and they shall beat their swords into plowshares,
> and their spears into pruning hooks;
> nation shall not lift up sword against nation,
> neither shall they learn war any more. (Mic. 4:3)

For generations we have sent missionaries to the African continent. One by one the peoples there have recently gained their freedom. If we believe the message we have been sending them, why not apply it now in our relations with the newer nations! Why not make that same demand of other strong nations. Even as the Christ of the Andes has been a dramatic symbol for peace and justice between two South American nations, can he not be the cementing bond between strong and weak nations? O America, let your prayer be not that profits might come, or prestige, or power, but that between the nations God's kingdom may come, God's will be done.

While a few with admirable commitment strive for the kingdom's coming in race relations, societal concerns, and international relations, the masses are lukewarm. They are for its coming—but not yet. Too many will consider God's agenda only after completing their own.

Though it may be a divine far-off event, God's rule will prevail. The last shall be first and the first last. The kingdom of this world shall become the kingdom of our God and of his Christ. In his mercy God permits and challenges us to be a part of this glorious consummation. So we join with one who prayed, "Let thy kingdom come—beginning with me."

A CONQUERING FAITH

BENJAMIN E. MAYS

President Emeritus of Morehouse College
Atlanta, Georgia

Faith is not blind chance. It is not ignorance. It is not a leap in the dark. It is not the opposite of reasoning nor the rejection of scientific data. Faith is partial understanding and the necessity and the urgency of taking the next step.

Faith is a commitment to something big, to something noble, to something worthwhile, to something that's all-embracing and all-consuming. Faith is a belief that this is right, though it can never be proved with scientific accuracy nor with mathematical certainty. Faith is belief in an ideal that you know is real but which you also know will never be attained. Faith is a belief that, however rocky the road, however thorny the path, tomorrow things will be better.

Faith is taking the next necessary step and leaving the consequences to God. That's faith.

Preceding an act of faith, we bring to bear upon the situation all the facts at our disposal, all the moral insight we can muster, all the reasoning we can command, all the religious experience through which we have passed; and then, having brought all that to bear on the situation, we act, trusting God for the results. That's faith!

If this is an adequate definition of faith, then there is no conflict between faith and knowledge, between faith and scientific data. The scientist needs faith. The business man needs faith. The statesman needs faith. In fact, no man can live without faith.

But I want to talk especially about the faith of a Palestinian Jew who could go to the cross and say while dying, "Father, into thy hands I commend my spirit." That took plenty of faith. Why didn't Jesus escape the cross and save himself?

He might have escaped if he had followed the Devil's advice! Said the Devil to Jesus: "Stake your life on things: bread, economic security, the material resources of the earth; worship power, prestige, position; appeal to the spectacular and get the public eye—do these things young man, and you will be great."

Or Jesus might have escaped the cross if he had obeyed the Pharisees, or the Sadducees, or the Zealots. The Pharisees said to him: "The way to make it is to conform to the status quo; keep the law, to the dotting of the *i*'s and the crossing of the *t*'s. The Sadducees urged him to observe correct procedure. The Zealots advised him to join the left-wing radicals and pull off a revolution. Any one of these methods might have saved Jesus from death on the cross. Why didn't Jesus do it? He *couldn't* do it.

Whoever seeks to live in conformity to the will of God can never completely conform to the will of man, can never completely abide by the mores of society and peers. There is tension between the authority of man and the authority of God. And when man moves under the authority of God, he moves not so much because he wants to move; he moves because he *must* move. He has no choice but to act.

Men inspired to write, to paint, to speak out, to prophesy, to act, do so because they must. There is an inner urge, an inner compulsion that drives them on. Such men understand what I have in mind when I speak of an inner urge, an inner compulsion, that *made* Jesus act.

John Bunyan had that inner urge when he said, "I had to set aside the writing of sermons and other serious tracts in order to write *Pilgrim's Progress*." Horace had it when he exclaimed, "I cannot sleep at night because of the pressure of unwritten poetry." Hampden understands this urge when he says, "I must play Hamlet in order to keep a contract with my soul." Marian Anderson knows it; when I listened to her sing, I felt that I was listening to one whom God Almighty sent into the world for the express purpose of singing. Amos experienced it when he cried out, "When the eternal God speaks who can but prophesy?" Jeremiah understood it when he said, "I feel there is a fire shut up in my bones." Paul knew it when he said, "I am ruined, literally ruined if I preach not the gospel." Ridley and Latimer knew the divine urge when they said just before being burned at the stake, "We will light a torch in England today that will never be put out." Jesus expressed it when he declared, "The spirit of the Lord is upon me because he hath anointed me to preach the gospel to the poor; he hath sent me to heal the broken-hearted, to preach deliverance to the captives, and recovering of sight to the blind, to set at liberty them that are bruised, to preach the acceptable year of the Lord." Martin Luther King, Jr. knew it full well when he said, "I have seen the promised land."

Acting on faith, acting on the urgency and the necessity to take the next step, Jesus dies with these words on his lips, "Father, into thy hands I commend my spirit." That's faith—taking the next step and leaving the consequences to God.

Was Jesus mistaken in leaving the consequences to God? Was he an impractical dreamer? An idealist? A fanatic? A man obsessed with a silly idea? Was he?

We turn to history. No, Jesus was not mistaken: Three days after the Resurrection the news got abroad that Jesus was alive again. The discouraged disciples who had gone back to their former occupations rallied around him again. A few days later Peter stood up at Pentecost and declared that this same Jesus "whom ye have taken and crucified" has been lifted up and made both Lord and Christ. And from this experience sprang the Christian church to hold up the name of the crucified Christ.

And all the way from Stephen to the present time, millions have died for him. More books have been written about him than any other, more songs have been composed about him than any other. More churches and cathedrals have been built in his name than any other. Jesus is today more vital than all the generals that ever marched, more awesome than all the kings that ever ruled, more powerful than all the presidents who ever sat. Even Napoleon admitted: "The more I study the world, the more I am convinced of the inability of force to create anything durable.

Alexander, Caesar, Charlemagne, and even I myself have founded empires, but upon what did they depend? They depended upon force." But Jesus Christ built his empire upon love and until this day millions will die for him.

The forces that crucified Jesus have passed away. The Roman Empire is gone. The barbarian hordes, the scribes, the Pharisees, the Sadducees, and the Zealots have all passed into history. The great British Empire is gone. But the crucified Christ is alive, still haunting men.

And the only hope for the world today *is* the crucified Christ. Across nineteen centuries he speaks to the world telling men and women that love and not hate is the way, peace and not war is the way, forgiveness and not revenge is the way, brotherhood and not caste is the way. Alcohol, homicide, dope, and crime—these are not the way. The Jesus way is the only hope for man.

No, Jesus was not mistaken. By losing his life he saved it.

But that is not the problem. It is easy to talk about the faith of a Palestinian Jew who died nineteen centuries ago. That's easy, the problem is—can we today appropriate the faith of Jesus? Can *we* commend our spirits to God?

Can we trust God, while we prepare for war, building the largest army, the most powerful navy, the biggest bombers, and spending billions on atomic, biological, and chemical implements of war? Can we do these things and still have faith in God? Can we? Can we dedicate ourselves to these ends and at the same time love God?

Can we develop our minds and at the same time develop our hearts, so that we will not only have learned men but good men? Can we develop in our colleges and universities intellectual giants without developing atheists, men who deny God? Can we develop men who believe in a scientific universe and who also believe in a moral universe? Can we?

Can we develop such faith in God that we will believe and live the doctrine that each and every soul of whatever race or nation is sacred unto God? And that when we hurt man, we hurt God? Can we?

If we cannot do this then our church services are vain; all our preaching is vain. If we cannot do this then our teaching is useless; all our great wealth is void; and all our scientific knowledge will lead eventually to catastrophe. For it was true many centuries ago and it is true now that "except the Lord build the house, they labor in vain that build it; except the Lord keep the city, the watchman waketh but in vain."

Faith is taking the next step and leaving the consequences to God. What will happen to me if I take the next step, do that which I know is right? What will happen to my job, to my family, to my prestige, to my political future—to my economic advancement? I do not know.

But I leave the consequences to God. I know only that I cannot drift beyond his love and care. I know only what Robert Browning expressed in his declaration of faith:

> One who never turned his back but marched breast forward,
> Never doubted clouds would break,
> Never dreamed, though right were worsted, wrong would triumph,
> Held we fall to rise, are baffled to fight better,
> Sleep to wake.

I know only what James Russell Lowell knew when he said in "The Present Crisis":

> Once to every man and nation comes the moment to decide,
> In the strife of Truth with Falsehood, for the good or evil side;
> Some great cause, God's new Messiah offering each the bloom or blight,
> Parts the goats upon the left hand, and the sheep upon the right;
> And the choice goes by forever 'twixt that darkness and that light. . . .
> Truth forever on the scaffold, Wrong forever on the throne.
> Yet that scaffold sways the future, and, behind the dim unknown,
> Standeth God within the shadow, keeping watch above his own.

Faith is taking the next step and leaving the consequences to God.

THE DRUM MAJOR INSTINCT

MARTIN LUTHER KING, JR.
(1929–1968)

Nobel Peace Prize Laureate;
President, Southern Christian Leadership Conference;
Co-Pastor of Ebenezer Baptist Church
Atlanta, Georgia

The text is taken from a very familiar passage recorded in the 10th chapter of Mark, beginning with the 35th verse.

The setting is clear. James and John are making a specific request of the Master. They had dreamed, as most of the Hebrews had dreamed, of a coming king of Israel who would set Jerusalem free and establish his kingdom on Mount Zion, and in righteousness rule the world. And they thought of Jesus as this kind of king, and they were thinking of that day when Jesus as this new King of Israel would reign supreme over Israel, and they were saying, "Now when you establish your kingdom, let one of us sit on the right hand and the other on the left hand of your throne."

Now very quickly, we would automatically condemn James and John. We would say they were selfish. Why would they make such a selfish request? But before we condemn them too quickly, let us look calmly and honestly at ourselves and we will discover that we, too, have those same basic desires for recognition, for importance—that same desire for attention, that same desire to be first.

Of course, the other disciples got mad at James and John, and you could understand why, but we must understand that we have some of the same "John and James qualities."

There is, deep down within all of us, an instinct—a kind of drum major instinct—a desire to be out front, a desire to lead the parade, a desire to be first. It is something that runs the whole gamut of life. And so before we condemn them, let us see that we all have the drum major instinct. We all want to be important, to surpass others, to achieve distinction, to lead the parade.

Alfred Adler, the great psychoanalyst, contends that this is the dominant impulse. Sigmund Freud used to contend that sex was the dominant impulse, and Adler came with a new argument saying that this quest for recognition, this desire for attention, this desire for distinction is the basic impulse—the basic drive of human life is this drum major instinct.

And you know, we begin early to ask life to put us first. Our first cry as a baby is a bid for attention, and all through childhood the drum major impulse, or instinct, is a major obsession. Children ask life to grant them first place. They are little bundles of ego. They have innately the drum major instinct.

Now in adult life we still have it and we really never get by it. We like to do something good, and you know we like to be praised for it. Now if you don't believe that, you just go on living life and you will discover very soon that you like to be praised.

Everybody likes it, as a matter of fact. And somehow this warm glow we feel when we are praised or when our name is in print is something like a "Vitamin A" to our ego. None of us is unhappy when we are praised, even if we know we don't deserve it and even if we don't believe it. People are unhappy about praise only when that praise is going too much towards somebody else. Everybody likes to be praised, because of this drum major instinct.

Do you know that a lot of the race problem grows out of the drum major instinct—a need that some people have to feel superior, a need that some people have to feel that they are first, to feel that their white skin ordains them to be first? And they have said that over and over again, in ways that we see with our own eyes. In fact, not too long ago a man down in Mississippi said that God was a charter member of the White Citizens Council. Well, if God is a charter member that gives everybody who belongs a kind of divinity, a kind of superiority. And think of what has happened in history as a result of this perverted use of the drum major instinct. It has led to the most tragic prejudice, to the most tragic expressions of man's inhumanity to man.

And not only does this thing go into the racial struggle, it goes into the struggle between nations. And I would submit to you this morning that what is wrong in the world today is that the nations of the world are engaged in a bitter, colossal contest for supremacy, and if something doesn't happen to stop this trend, I'm sorely afraid that we won't be here to talk about Jesus Christ and about God and about brotherhood too many more years.

If somebody doesn't bring an end to this suicidal thrust that we see in the world today, none of us is going to be around, because somebody's going to make the mistake through our senseless blundering of dropping a nuclear bomb somewhere, and then another one is going to drop. And don't let anybody fool you: this can happen within a matter of seconds. They have twenty-megaton bombs in Russia right now that can destroy a city as big as New York in three seconds, with everybody wiped away, and every building! And we can do the same thing to Russia and China.

This is where we have drifted, and we are drifting there because nations are caught up with the drum major instinct: "I must be first, I must be supreme, our nation must rule the world."

And I am sad to say that the nation in which we live is the supreme culprit, and I'm going to continue to say it to America, because I love this country too much to see it drift along the path it has taken.

God didn't call America to do what we're doing in the world now. God didn't call America to engage in a senseless, unjust war as the war in Vietnam. We are criminals in that war, we have committed more war crimes almost than any nation in the world, and I'm going to continue to say it.

We won't stop it because of our pride and our arrogance as a nation, but God has a way of even putting nations in their place. The God that I worship has a way of saying, "Don't play with me." He has a way of saying, as the God of the Old Testament used to say to the Hebrews, "Don't play with me, don't play with me, Babylon. Be still and know that I am God. If you don't stop your reckless course, I'll rise up and break the backbone of your power."

And that can happen to America. Every now and then I go back and read Gibbon's *Decline and Fall of the Roman Empire.* And when I come and look at America I say to myself, "The parallels are frightening. We have perverted the drum major instinct."

But let me rush on to my conclusion because I want you to see what Jesus was really saying to James and John.

What was the answer that Jesus gave these men? It's very interesting. One would have thought that Jesus would have condemned them. One would have thought that Jesus would have said: "You are out of your place. You're selfish. Why would you raise such a question?" But that isn't what Jesus did.

He did something altogether different. He said, in substance: "Oh, I see. You want to be first. You want to be great. You want to be important. You want to be significant. Well, you ought to be. If you want to be my disciple, you *must* be."

Jesus reordered priorities. He said, "Yes, don't give up this instinct. It's a good instinct if you use it right. It's a good instinct if you don't distort it and pervert it. Don't give it up. Keep feeling the need for being important. Keep feeling the need for being first. But I want you to be first in love, I want you to be first in moral excellence, I want you to be first in generosity. That is what I want you to do."

He transformed the situation by giving a new definition of greatness. And you know how he said it? He said, "Now, brethren, I can't give you greatness, and really I can't make you first." This is what Jesus said to James and John. "You must earn it. True greatness comes not by favoritism but by fitness. And the right hand and the left are not mine to give. They belong to those who are prepared."

And so Jesus gave us a new norm of greatness. If you want to be important, wonderful. If you want to be recognized, wonderful.

If you want to be great, wonderful. But recognize that he who is greatest among you shall be your servant.

That's a new definition of greatness, and this morning the thing that I like about that definition of greatness is that it means that everybody can be great, because everybody can serve. Every now and then I guess we all think realistically about that day when we will be victimized with what is life's final common denominator, that something we call death.

We all think about it, and every now and then I think about my own death and I think about my own funeral, and I don't think of it in a morbid sense. Every now and then I ask myself what is it that I would want said, and I leave the word to you this morning.

If any of you are around when I have to meet may day, I don't want a long funeral. And if you get somebody to deliver the eulogy, tell him not to talk too long. Every now and then I wonder what I want them to say.

Tell them not to mention that I have a Nobel Peace Prize; that isn't important. Tell them not to mention that I have three or four hundred other awards; that's not important. Tell them not to mention where I went to school.

I'd like somebody to mention, that day, that "Martin Luther King, Jr. tried to give his life serving others." I'd like for somebody to say, that day, that "Martin Luther King, Jr. tried to love somebody." I want you to be able to say, that day, that I tried to be right on the war question. I want you to be able to say that I did try to feed the hungry. And I want you to be able to say, that day, that I did try in my life to clothe those who were naked. I want you to say on that day that I did try in my life to visit those who were in prison. I want you to say that I tried to love and serve humanity.

Yes, if you want to say that I was a drum major, say that I was a drum major for justice, say that I was a drum major for peace, that I was a drum major for righteousness.

And all of the other shallow things will not matter. I won't have any money to leave behind. I won't have the fine and luxurious things of life to leave behind. But I just want to leave a committed life behind. And that's all I want to say.

> If I can help somebody as I pass along,
> If I can cheer somebody with a word or song,
> If I can show somebody he's traveling wrong,
> Then my living will not be in vain.
> If I can do my duty as a Christian ought,
> If I can bring salvation to a world once wrought,
> If I can spread the message as the Master taught,
> Then my living will not be in vain.

Yes, Jesus, I want to be on your right side or your left side, but not for any selfish reason. I want to be on your right or left side, not in terms of some political kingdom or ambition. I just want to be there in love and in justice and in truth.

TOWARD THE MARK OF
THE HIGH CALLING

MARTIN LUTHER KING, SR.

*Pastor Emeritus of Ebenezer Baptist Church
Atlanta, Georgia*

> Brethren, I count not myself to have apprehended: but this
> one thing I do, forgetting those things which are behind, and
> reaching forth unto those things which are before, I press
> toward the mark for the prize of the high calling of God in
> Christ Jesus.
>
> —Philippians 3:13–14

I want to deal with three familiar concerns: retrospection, introspection, and prospection.

Retrospection refers to those things that have passed. In the
text, Paul commands us to forget those things of the past. There
are some things that I don't want to remember, things I have encountered in my lifetime, things that are hard to forget. We have
all heard people say, "I will forgive you, but I won't forget the
things you have done." But I know from personal experience that
it is possible to forget. However, if you are to forget, you cannot
keep malice and hatred in your heart toward another person. And,
if you cannot forget the evil he has done to you, then you cannot
forgive him. We must, therefore, get rid of the evil, malice, and
hatred we have in our hearts toward people that have wronged us.
We must forgive if we are to "forget those things that are behind."

Now there are some things that we shouldn't forget. For instance, I remember when I became a Christian. I often think back

46

on that day when I was converted and it makes me feel good. There is nothing wrong with retrospection so long as it doesn't keep us from looking forward.

But before thinking about moving forward let us reflect for a moment on introspection. Introspection means to examine one's own thoughts and feelings. It makes us look on the inside of ourselves. Jesus challenges each of us to do this. He spoke of dealing with the log in my own eye before worrying too much about the speck in my neighbor's eye. Before raising a question about someone else we should always raise a question about ourselves. How am I doing morally? What are my strengths and my weaknesses? What am I to do with myself?

I raised these questions the other day in Los Angeles, California when I had an unusual experience with my wife who is now deceased. While reflecting on her and the life we shared together I felt her spirit and presence with me. She stayed with me all night, and walked down a strange road. She said to me, "I'm glad that you can walk better now," and I asked her, "Honey, where is this road going?" She then said, "This road is going to give out." What does this mean? Does it mean that this body of mine is giving out? Or, does it have something to say about prospection?

Prospection refers to the future. Retrospection shows us the things that have shaped our lives, and we begin to realize that we can never know what we are or what we ought to be until we understand the tradition out of which we have come. But forgetting those negative parts of our experience which are behind us, as Paul says, we press forward toward the mark of the high calling in Christ. My retrospection and introspection suggest that I should press forward, and not only I but we as a people should press forward. And where are we going? We are bound for the promised land.

We don't know what the future holds for us, but we do know that we are not alone. The Lord has been with us in the past. He is with us presently. And he will be with us in the future. Things get difficult for us sometimes. Sometimes we have to cry, walk the floor at night, and question a lot of things. But in spite of it all we must have the firm conviction that God is with us.

We look toward the future believing that things are going to get better. And when this road of life gives out, as I was reminded in my moments of reflection on the death of my wife, we move out of temporality into eternality, out of finitude into infinitude, and out of mortality into immortality.

JESUS AND HIS CHURCH

JOSEPH A. JOHNSON, JR.

Presiding Bishop, Fourth Episcopal District
of the Christian Methodist Episcopal Church
Shreveport, Louisiana

> Now when Jesus came into the district of Caesarea Philippi,
> he asked his disciples, "Who do men say that the Son of
> man is?" And they said, "Some say John the Baptist, others
> say Elijah, and others Jeremiah or one of the prophets." He
> said to them, "But who do you say that I am?" Simon Peter
> replied, "You are the Christ, the Son of the living God."
> And Jesus answered him, "Blessed are you, Simon Bar-
> Jona! For flesh and blood has not revealed this to you, but
> my Father who is in heaven."
>
> —Matthew 16:13–17

Here we have the story of another withdrawal which Jesus made.
The end was coming very near, and Jesus needed as much time
as possible alone with his disciples. He had so much to say to
them, so much to teach them, even though there were many
things which they could not then bear, could not yet understand.
In order to be with his disciples he withdrew to the district of
Caesarea Philippi.

Confronting Jesus at this crucial moment—as his time was
running out—was one clamant and demanding problem: Was
there anyone who understood him? Was there anyone who had
recognized him for who and what he was? Were there any who,
when he was gone from the flesh, would carry on his work and
labor for his kingdom? Obviously this was a critical question. At
stake was the very survival of the Christian faith. If there was

49

none who had grasped the truth, or even glimpsed it, then all his work was undone; if there were at least a few who had grasped it, his work was safe. So Jesus as determined to put all to the test, and to ask his followers who they believed him to be.

It is of the most dramatic interest to see where Jesus chose to ask this fateful question. There have been few places with more diverse and pronounced religious associations than Caesarea Philippi.

The area was crowded with temples of the ancient Syrian Baal worship. There were fifteen temples in the near neighborhood. Ancient religion breathed in the very air and atmosphere of the place. It was here in Baal's territory that Jesus asked the question, "Who do men say that I the Son of man am?"

Nor were the Syrian gods the only ones worshipped there. Near Caesarea Philippi there rose a great hill, in which was a deep cavern; and that cavern was said to be the birthplace of the great god with whom Caesarea Philippi was so closely identified, the god whose original name was Paneas—and to this day the place is known as Banias. Here surrounded by the gods of Greece, Jesus asked the question, "Who do men say that I the Son of man am?"

But there was something more. In Caesarea Philippi there was a great temple of white marble built to the godhead of Caesar. No one could look at Caesarea Philippi, even from a distance, without seeing that pile of glistening marble, and thinking of the might of Rome and the divinity of the emperor.

Here then indeed is a dramatic picture of the homeless, penniless Galilean carpenter with twelve very ordinary men around him. At the moment the orthodox people of his day are actually plotting and planning to eliminate and to destroy him as a dangerous heretic, he stands in an area littered with the temples of the Syrian gods, in a place where the ancient Greek gods looked down, where the white marble splendor of the home of Caesarworship dominated the landscape and compelled the eye. And here, of all places, this amazing carpenter stands and asks men who they believe him to be—and expects the answer, the Son of God. It is as if Jesus deliberately set himself against the background of the world's religions in all their history and all their splendor, and demanded to be compared with them—and to have the verdict given in his favor.

Jesus appears to be saying, "Whatever the gods of Syria may have, and the gods of Greece, and even of imperial Rome, I have more. I have light for your darkness, knowledge for your ignorance, life for your existence, peace for your souls, and victory for your defeats."

There is drama also in the answers to his question, "Who do men say that I the Son of man am?" Notice first that the disciples, with a fine delicacy, do not report the idle and thoughtless gossip of the evil-minded slander of the day. There were some critics who said that he was a glutton and a winebibber. Many mocked him as a friend of publicans and sinners. Some sneered at him as the carpenter turned prophet. Others surmised that he was a political enthusiast. Still others regarded him as a simple and dreamy mystic. The disciples ignored all these ill-judged and occasionally venomous characterizations. They reported rather only the serious talk they had heard in the marketplace, at the supper table, and at the door of the synagogue.

"Some say that you are John the Baptist." This was the view of many who had heard of John the Baptist and remembered the religious awakening under his preaching. What the people found common to both Jesus and John was the note of fearlessness and absolute sincerity. John the Baptist was a preacher, and the people appeared to be saying, "In spite of all the differences between you and John the Baptist, both of you are preachers of the gospel."

Jesus was a preacher. From his lips came gems of literature, words of healing and life, messages of comfort and cheer, the good news of God's kingdom. Jesus preached until men felt that their sins were forgiven and their lives cleansed. Jesus preached until the storms in men's lives were quieted and the surging billows of passion and emotion were tamed. Jesus preached until lame men got up and walked, and scales fell from the eyes of the blind. Jesus preached until men threw away their crutches and dead men got out of their graves. Jesus was a preacher!

This preaching is something that every preacher ought to have in common with Jesus. I think the most serious and most damaging charge that can be brought against a preacher is that he cannot preach. He knows how to work with the Boy Scouts, he can lead in a public demonstration, he can march in a civil rights protest, but the man can't preach! What a tragedy! And what a denial of the ministry of Jesus!

"Others say Elijah." The purpose of Jesus Christ was so plainly to call men to a new faith in God, and a new life, that some believed he must be that Elijah who should appear before the King came to restore the kingdom to his people. They remembered that Jesus proclaimed the coming of the kingdom, that he cleansed the temple, that he healed the widow's son, that he fearlessly rebuked the hypocrisy of the scribes and Pharisees, that he paid no deference to those who sat in high places—and they passed their verdict on him that he was Elijah.

Jesus and Elijah had something in common. On Mount Carmel Elijah had confronted Israel with a decision. Elijah said to the crowd, "If God be God, then follow him. And if Baal be God then follow *him*. Put the matter to a test: the god that answers by fire, let him be God." As Elijah confronted the crowd with a decision about God, so Jesus confronts men with a decision about himself.

Jesus confronts men with a decision. You must make a decision! You cannot remain the same when you come in contact with him. Jesus appears to be saying to the world, "If the gods of Greece be God, if the gods of the Caesar-Baal worship be God, if the gods of Rome be God, well, then follow them. But if you want to know who God is and what God is doing, look at my ministry and my concern for the poor and wretched of the earth."

John the Baptist once sent his delegation from prison to ask, "Are you the Christ or shall we look for another?" Jesus responded, in effect: "Well, that question demands an existential answer. It cannot be answered philosophically and academically. You go back and tell John what is happening around here! Go back and tell him: The lame are walking! The blind are seeing! The gospel is preached to the poor! The deaf are hearing! And the dead are being raised! Go back and tell John!"

"Others Jeremiah." It is easy to understand why many passed the verdict that Jesus Christ was a second Jeremiah: they saw him as a man of compassion. They heard him sigh when he healed the dumb. They noted his constant protest against the unbelieving authorities of his day. They discerned the sorrow which dwelt in his eyes when men turned back from him and mocked at his prophecies. They saw him weep at the grave of Lazarus. They saw him moved with compassion when the widow of Nain lost her only son. They saw the care, concern, and compassion which he had for all people.

The Greek word "to have compassion" means literally, as Karl Barth has pointed out, that Jesus buries himself in the concern, the misery, and the troubles of the people. He identifies himself with everybody who has a burden to bear. He takes on the weaknesses of men, their limitations, heartaches, sorrows, and anxieties. His heart and message go out to the nobodies of the world, men and women who are written off by the world, people who do not count, people who have been pushed to the limits of their existence. It was the common people who heard him gladly, who followed him and hung on every word that fell from his lips. Then as now, Jesus continues to identify himself with the common, ordinary people.

"Or one of the prophets." This was the wisest and most discerning of the four reported verdicts. Jesus was to these men a teacher come from God, another of that sublime succession which began with Moses and continued through such great names as Samuel, Nathan, Amos, Hosea, and Isaiah—the long line of lonely and heroic men who spoke the word of the Lord. This is the verdict most common among the best minds of our own age, among discerning people not yet within the Christian church. Jesus Christ is to them the prophet of humanity. His wisdom, his purity, his insight, the reach and grasp of his thought, the depth and pathos of his words, the unique simplicity of his teaching—all evoke their glowing eulogies. They know that he is not the Christ of the ascetic, or of the democratic reformer who—although he denies His claims—would use Christ to multiply the loaves and fishes, or of the tender sentimentalists for whom Christ is a figure to idealize. But precisely as these wise and thoughtful observers fell pitiably below a true conception of the Christ, and what he came to do, so their modern successors fall far below the true conception of him who came not merely to teach but to redeem. Jesus is more than John the Baptist, more than Elijah, more than Jeremiah, more than one of the prophets. Preacher and teacher, fearless and compassionate, he is all of this, and more. And that "more" is the mystery which gives life to his church, and finds such dramatic expression on the lips and in the lives of those who are truly his disciples.

A DRINK OF WATER FROM HOME: THE MINISTRY OF IDENTITY

HENRY H. MITCHELL

Director of the Ecumenical Center for Black Church Studies Claremont, California

A great concern of mine as I think of my home church in Columbus, Ohio—and others like it—is the question of just what the blessings of God unto blacks of several generations have wrought. It is the question of what happens to people who hear the word and who pursue a higher education and are thus able to engage in upward mobility—able to live and act more and more like the white middle class of America. The question is especially important among our young people, because they, not unlike the so-called hippie generation of white Americans, have come to consider the achievements of American affluence as a kind of dust and ashes in our hands. It might be well, therefore, for us who have gone this route to stop for a few moments and ponder this question—to think about who we are.

I should like to call to your attention 1 Chronicles 11:17, our text, "And David longed, and said, 'Oh, that somebody would give me a drink of water from the well at Bethlehem, the one that is down by the gate.'" David's wistful sigh is part of a rich story deserving of our repeated attention.

David was fleeing, as it were, from Saul. He was not anxious to conquer Saul, but not anxious either to be murdered by Saul's accomplices. David was also in the midst of the Philistines, and while he was an extremely skillful, courageous, and in fact successful guerila chieftain, he was, like all guerillas, in a decided minority. He was able to win many small battles and make many successful strikes in enemy territory, but because of the limited size of his force he could never "win the war." Always he had to hit and run; and no matter how many strikes he made, he was never able to relax and feel that he had won the decisive and final victory. It was a taxing kind of existence, this never-ending warfare. David was always aware that he was in the minority, and that the Philistines out there were big and "bad." And so he almost never rested, and when he did it was all too short.

Our text finds him in the cave of Adullam, surrounded by Philistines who do not even know he is there. He stretches out on a rock, sweaty, tired, and almost completely discouraged. In his fatigue and low spirits he longingly cries out, "I wish somebody would bring me a cup of water from the spring back home in Bethlehem, the one by the gate."

Some of David's most courageous warriors heard that cry, and they knew just how much it meant, so they sneaked through the lines, went right to Philistine headquarters, got the water, and brought it back. When they gave David the water, he was so moved that he poured it out as a libation, in the manner of our African ancestors. He said, "This is, as it were, the blood of these heroes, and I dare not drink it." So he poured it upon the ground as an offering to God.

One has to wonder what was in David's mind when he cried out for that water, for his subsequent act of worship obviously rules out mere *physical* thirst. There was no literal indication that his body would respond better to that special water, drawn from a particular spring at a little town named Bethlehem. David was really saying that he had need of physical and *spiritual* refreshment. He was saying in effect: "I need something to get myself back together. When I was a boy tending my father's flocks, I used to come in from the fields—from the dangers of lions and bears—tense and hot and tired, and suddenly I would step inside the safety of the gate, away from the taxing responsibility, and I'd get a drink of water. And oh, how it would refresh me! I need now something like what that little town and spring gave." There in the cave of Adullam David was saying that he longed for that same safety from the enemy, that same respite from tension, that same acceptance and love and support which always awaited him in Bethlehem with his Daddy, Jesse, and the rest of the family.

Perhaps in a more subtle and profound way, David was also recalling the reaffirmation of his very selfhood which came with being in Bethlehem. It was here that he had first become a person, and no matter that in the minds of some Bethlehem was the "least" of all the towns in Judah—it was *home.* That was where David first became somebody; and every time he thought about Bethlehem and all it did to make him a person, he celebrated that little town and was healed by the thought.

What does this mean for all of us? I would hope that it might help us to remember who *we* are, since nobody can act effectively who does not know and embrace who he or she is, including "where you are from." We *are* whoever *we* are, *from* where we are *from,* and not where we *wish* we were from.

I used to pastor on the West Coast, and I was always asking people where they were from. It seemed nosy, but I was really just seeking ways to relate to them. We had many members from Louisiana, and when I'd ask the usual question Do you know so-and-so? they'd say, "No, I'm from Shreveport." But I'd learn later that they were from Cushata, or Robinson, or some little town like that. Or some would say, "We are from New Orleans." And I'd ask who was pastor of their church, only to find that they were from Gretna, or Lutcher, or Garyville, or Slidell, or some place like that. Now they might have said—or meant—"*near* New Orleans," but that wasn't what came out. The impact of their words was very different. It seemed as if they were ashamed of the very place that gave them breath. Well, you can't be renewed and live with fear or uncertainty like that. If you can't respect the place you are from, you certainly can't respect the person from that place. To embrace the person you must embrace the place. If God made you in Cushata, thank God for Cushata and be healed.

David was saying, "I can't wait until I conquer the Philistines to respect myself." It may be that we have a few Cadillacs and fine homes, but we are still amidst the Philistines. And if we can't be "who we are," we aren't anything. David's cry helps us to accept and indeed to celebrate our selfhood.

I think of two people I have talked with in recent years, one a woman of great talent. At her best she was, and still could be, a top professional, but she had become an alcoholic. Her behavior was horrible beyond belief, until I discovered that underneath it all was an inability to accept herself as black, a yearning to become acceptable by being white. She had tried to get away from her nature and her origins. But she failed, and there wasn't enough alcohol anywhere to cure her problem.

The other person I think of was a member of my parish years ago. Now at age thirty-three, he is high up in a major multinational corporation, and going higher. But when I visit his expensive home outside New York City and sit on the shore of his large and private lake, I am at peace, because he talks about the days he and our son cut grapes for raisins, and the days he picked cotton. He seems to glory in the memory of dust and bee bites in California's San Joaquin Valley. My visits are for him a reminder of who he is and where he's from, and that is far more important than the heights to which he has risen in the Philistine world. Our often hilarious reminiscences are for him a drink of water from home.

This is what the black church is about, in part. Our religion ought to be a celebration in which we look back and wonder how we got over as far as we did. We can't thank God for final victory because there is so much oppression still, but we can thank him for making us who we are, and we can be at peace.

The Jews have a religious celebration in which they make shacks out of branches in memory of their slavery in Egypt and the exodus of more than three thousand years ago. I used to watch the celebration every year as it took place just across from my own seminary in New York City. Ph.D.'s, high officials, and millionaires came together solemnly and dramatically to remember the slavery of their ancestors and the bondage of their people even now. This remembrance of who they are has been a source of great strength for them in the face of great obstacles. It has been like a drink of water from home.

In like manner the black church has been and is a place where we could be who we are, and act like we act, and praise God like we praise God. We have known that there we could shout and, as the spiritual says, "Ain't nobody there gonna turn you out." The black church has been our refuge, our place to be who we are. Here we have found total acceptance, with our family and extended kin. Here we have received our drink of water from home.

No longer does anyone have to sneak through lines, or hide from ol' massa our nourishing celebration. No longer do we suffer from the illusion that we have to praise God in a way that pleases a majority power group. But there is still a problem. Now that the danger is not so obvious, the problem is that we may think the battle over and forget to drink the water.

We must *never* forget that power comes with the healing of the drink, the strength of planting real feet on the real earth. No matter what our salary or position, no matter how busy we are or how much in demand, every one of us is still a guerilla in a hostile world. And God can't use us unless we are what he made us. The higher we rise, the more we have to concentrate on getting that drink of water from home.

I thank God for a host of young blacks in the most prestigious colleges of our land who have not been fooled by acceptances, by admissions, and even scholarships. They continue to sense their need for that life-giving drink of water. The girls at Smith College have a great gospel choir to keep them "together." Recently I went to Los Angeles to hear the Black Ensemble from Oberlin, and what a feast it was! In the midst of the Philistines they had learned to sing the songs of their Zion and be healed.

A few years ago a law school student appeared for worship in her church in Cambridge, Massachusetts. She had to plead her first case in moot court the next day. Her friends wanted to know why she was there in church instead of over at the library researching cases and refining her brief. Her answer was that she couldn't dream of tackling so great a task without "getting herself together" in healing fellowship with her Lord and his people. She stayed there in the church all that Sunday, singing and praising God. Apparently it paid off. The next morning the real person was in fact "together" there in the pleadings, and the professor afterward told her she was a *born* trial lawyer. When he later learned she was a black preacher's kid, he also said, "I should have known it!" For even the Philistines respect the Davids who are nourished and refreshed by that drink of water from home.

DELIVERANCE IN SEARCH OF UNITY

JOHN T. WALKER

Suffragan Bishop of the Episcopal Church
Washington, D.C.

Much has been heard recently in America about the beginnings of the nation. All over the land, in drama, art, music, and even religion, people have recalled the ringing words of Thomas Jefferson and Patrick Henry, and celebrated deliverance from the tyranny of George III. The early settlers have been praised for their courageous pioneering, and the founding fathers for having found a way to unity—unity of purpose, of being, and of meaning. For such unity was indispensable to a successful revolution. Without it a new nation could not have been born.

As we think about liberation and unity, and all the slogans that have marked the extended birthday celebration, we need to look deeply at the dream that underwrote the celebrated event and was to form the glue to hold the people together. We need to ask some hard questions about dream and reality, or, to put it differently, about substance and image.

A year or so before the Mayflower landed, the first black people arrived on these shores. From that moment on we have been a thorn in the flesh of the nation. The unity sought in the name itself has eluded the *United* States of America because so large a segment of its people were not included in either the deliverance or the liberation, much less the unity. From the beginning a lethal danger lurked in the inability to include all of humanity in the grand concept. Everyone knew, from the beginning, that even the Declaration of Independence and the subsequent Constitution did not mean what they said when they spoke of "all men"—and this knowledge caused a permanent split between what was being said and the life that was being lived.

This fractured integrity was dangerous because, as Jesus had long ago argued and Lincoln reminded us, a house divided against itself could not stand. And earlier, the Hebrew prophets had warned that the supposed day of celebration, the coming Day of the Lord, would not be a day of rejoicing but a day of pain and anguish. The *image* was of a great Day of freedom and justice for all, the *dream* was that of a "holy experience" in which all would be free and none seen as better than others. But the *reality* was a nation practicing the most terrible form of slavery and hypocrisy.

There is no need to spend much time on distant history. We all are well aware of what happened, and the degree to which it continues to happen. Rather what we need to do is to look at the impact of this split policy on the nation's place in the world and what it means for all of us. For example, how have immigration prejudices affected recent foreign policy?

The deliverance/liberation/unity theme with which the nation began was soon forgotten or lost, as the dream was compromised away. In its place the "melting pot," conceived as an amalgam "for whites only," became America's watchword. As immigration became a tool of national expansion and a source of cheap non-slave labor, the immigration laws became the chief means for excluding people of color. The latter part of the nineteenth century saw the first steps to exclude Orientals, which finally resulted in the Chinese Exclusion Act and the gentlemen's agreement to greatly limit Japanese immigration. The various quota schemes and the grandfather clause were designed to keep people of color out of the country and thus out of the melting pot. The new man who would control this new nation would be *white, blonde, blue-eyed.*

The end result of such a policy would be to destroy any lingering credibility the nation might have. Coupled with the internal black/white problem it would give the lie to the notion that America was a nation committed to the idea of liberation and unity. One wonders if it has influenced Chinese attitudes toward the United States.

Since 1954 we have been on a collision course with reality. Black America has been offering salvation to a reluctant people. And even as this was happening we have ourselves been searching for unity. When the liberation movement began, it was with a sense of deep religious commitment. With Martin Luther King, Jr. we saw ourselves as the modern-day people of God, destined not only for deliverance ourselves but also to be instruments in God's hands for the deliverance or liberation of the entire nation. But at every point battles were waged to prevent the fulfillment of the dream.

Given its religious roots, however, its basis in faith, the movement was not to be stopped. It could not be stopped because the leaders understood that, without a national homeland of our own to turn to, we needed something upon which to build unity. They knew what our forebears had known, that we cannot achieve liberation or deliverance without a unifying purpose. They knew what our Jewish brethren have always known, that deliverance out of Egypt was related to Moses and Yahweh in a unique way, that the development of the idea of a chosen people was no accident but necessary for the welding of the people into a community, and that only in community can the fulfillment of liberation and deliverance be found.

Throughout the history of the Hebrew people this has been demonstrated again and again. During the long periods of exile and dispersion it was their sense of unity as God's chosen people bearing the Ark of the Covenant that held them together. When religion diminishes in the life of the Jews, when traditionalism replaces the Ark of the Covenant, then the need for a nation/homeland becomes an absolute imperative. This is not to say that the desire for a homeland is less strong among those who are religious, but only that the faithful are able to survive and hope even in exile. Without Yahweh however, the people must have a political Israel.

Our black leadership, where it was wise, recognized the importance of religion in the very bones of the black people, for they knew that in the absence of political nationhood or a common language, all efforts at unity would fail. Unless the promises of God mediated through the Christ could become the source of unity and strength among us, we would perish under opposition. Thus the liberation movement would have a strong base and, if successful, the deliverance experience would have the depth and power to realize itself in all of our people. Through the fifties and early sixties this power was present. Then as the movement became increasingly secular it seemed less sure of itself. Rhetoric replaced that power which had motivated the people—and the movements and marches—and we began to lose that unity of purpose and direction which is so important to liberation at every point along the way.

The victory which we won, limited though it was, and for which a high price was paid in the blood of the martyrs and in the untold suffering of millions from 1619 to now, has lately seemed to lose ground. A new generation of young men and women have come along, many of them so disillusioned that they prefer, or seem to prefer, a life outside the systems we have maintained. Many of them are lost in ignorance, drugs, prostitution, gambling, and crime. Frequently our efforts to place young people in top positions in the secular world come to nothing because too often we still lack a reservoir of youth trained for many of the newer jobs. The dropout list is greater than ever, and even though we are educating more than ever before we still seem to be losing ground.

Are there answers? I think there are, but they are not to be found in the increased secularization of our people. If we are satisfied simply to emulate or imitate the split personality of America, then we will all fall together.

The answer is to be found rather in the ever strengthening power of a faith that calls us to share our knowledge—and share such wealth as we have—so that our young can be saved or restored. The answer is to develop pride of being—not self-centeredness but concerned love—so that we stop robbing and murdering one another. The answer is to educate ourselves and our young people in the faith of the fathers, that faith which opened them to receive the Divine Spirit and helped them to survive. It is the Spirit who causes old men to dream dreams and young men to see visions. It is he who has led us to pursue the dream of deliverance, and might yet give us that unity which alone can make deliverance a reality.

AFFLICTED, BUT NOT DEFEATED

J. DEOTIS ROBERTS, SR.

Professor of Theology
Howard University School of Religion
Washington, D.C.

Wherever we turn in the great literature of the human race, we come upon something that is common to the experience of all people. The writers and poets of every nation, period, and language have been able to articulate what is universally human. They show us ourselves—in all our frustration, perplexity, despair, anxiety, and persecution. They express what it feels like to be cast down and in need of hope, courage, and meaning in life.

I remember some years ago reading a Japanese story in which a woman was trapped for several days in the sand dunes, and the emotional experience of being trapped with no possibility of escape over a long period of time was indeed a traumatic experience for her. When we read in the novels of Dostoevsky concerning the notes of the underground we come upon similar deep currents in the Russian soul. Jean Paul Sartre's writings, in many ways, reflect this same kind of experience in French. Or, if we come to black literature and read Richard Wright, we find something quite similar. All people reflect—and write—out of the particularity of their existential experience, and yet there is in the great literature a commonality of human emotion.

Sometime ago I read a story in the literature of India. It spoke of a man who was being chased by a ferocious animal and fell into a well. As he slipped down the embankment he caught hold of a twig—and a worm was eating up the twig. As the man kept sliding ever deeper into the well he became aware of a giant snake, a python, at the bottom of the well just waiting to devour him. This is the way in which the Indian writer sought to describe the universal experience I am talking about. Paul put it well: We are troubled from every side and yet we are not distressed; we are persecuted but not forsaken; we are cast down but not destroyed.

The Old Testament, in the Book of Exodus, speaks about a people who went through just such an experience. The Israelites had been in bondage in Egypt. As the result of many mighty acts of God and the courageous leadership of Moses they were led to a passageway out of Egypt. Suddenly they reached the brink of the Red Sea. With Pharoah's army behind them, mountains on both sides, and the Red Sea in front of them, there seemed to be no way of escape. The people, therefore, began to criticize Moses—as many of us do our leaders—and they said to him "Were there no graves in Egypt that we could have died there? Why did you bring us here that we might perish?" At this point Moses became disturbed and cried unto God, and God said, "Moses, why do you cry unto me? What is it that you have in your hand? Stretch forth your rod." The thing that we can learn from this situation is that, so often, we ask God to do for us what we are capable of doing for ourselves. God has created us with freedom and responsibility; he has also given us many talents. We are the highest expression of God's creative power. Therefore, we are to go forth and make use of that which God has given us. And when we expect God to do for us what we are capable of doing for ourselves, God says to us, as he said to Moses, "What is it that you have in your hand?" We have a hand full of power and God wants us to use it.

Faith expresses itself in terms of the way in which we ought to be delivered, both as individuals and as a people. One of the wonderful things about the Old Testament is that it expresses itself in terms of Israel's collective self, its "corporate personality." Israel was a kind of prototype of what the church is as the family of God, the household of God, a fellowship of believers, the body of Christ.

For black people, the American situation has often been perceived as similar to Egyptian bondage. We have come forth unto God out of our affliction and suffering. And often we have expected God to do for us what we can do for ourselves. But God reminded us and he reminds us still that we have something in our midst that we must use. God is with us, and will remain with us; he says to us, "As I was with Moses so will I be with you." But his continued presence with us does not mean that we are to minimize our human efforts in the quest for complete freedom and humanization.

The faith of our black fathers and mothers is one that was expressed in the spiritual "Go down, Moses, 'way down in Egypt's land./ Tell ole Pharoah, to let my people go!" The message of this spiritual came through very clearly to the people who were oppressed and it comes through very clearly to us today. The message is that the same God who delivered the Israelites will also deliver our people. He will deliver us, however, only if we are able and willing to continue the fight for freedom, justice, and righteousness, doing what is in our hand to do.

And, although many of us are able to move up the ladder to the higher echelons of America society, let us not forget that we have not "made it" unless our *people* have come through. We must have the spirit of a young man who was in the law school of Yale University some time ago. When he got his degree from Yale he was offered an opportunity to become a lawyer on the staff of a great corporation. But he said, "Watts is my home, and until the people who live in that situation are free, I'm not free. And I have a calling to go back and serve my people." Wherever we go as blacks let us remember where we came from. And if some of us ascend to the heights of success, let us remember that we represent only a small number, because the majority of black people are sinking deeper and deeper in oppression, affliction, and misery. Our faith calls us to serve those who have not made it. This is our special calling.

In many ways America has been an experience for black Americans similar to the Egyptian experience of the Israelites. We have heard much lately about the American success story, the realization of the American dream, and the realization of the kingdom of God. But as a black people we have often seen this reality from the bottom up rather than from the top down. Therefore, our special calling is to those among us who are poor, afflicted, oppressed, and wounded. We should remember that Moses was entitled to the prerogatives of royalty in that he was an adopted son in Pharoah's house, but he chose instead to suffer affliction with the people of God. He had a sense of corporate personality, meaning that he was concerned with the oppressed of the land. This sense of corporate personality is what we need today.

We, as a black people, need to join hands in this spirit of corporate personality and move forward toward the eradication of social evils. The black church embodies this sense of corporate personality. It remains our last best hope. It is the only instrument of power we have left within the black community. It is the only institution we really own. Instead of standing outside the black church and criticizing it, we need to move inside and radicalize it. For wherever there is a structure of evil, there is need for a structure of righteousness to oppose it. The black church represents this structure of righteousness and calls upon us to use it.

This is the faith that has brought us this far, and it is the faith that is needed to take us further. This is the faith that has sustained us in our afflictions within this nation. This faith kept our communities and families together in spite of all of the problems we had to endure. This faith wouldn't allow us to shrink although we were oppressed by many. In the midst of grief and pain this faith kept alive our hope in a better future.

As a people we have majored in hope. We have hoped when there was no certain or empirical evidence that things were going to get better. We have transmitted this hope to our children and they are beginning to implement it. With this faith and hope we can join with the Apostle Paul in saying, "Even though we are afflicted, oppressed, and persecuted, we are not destroyed."

WHEN ATROPHY SETS IN

WILLIAM V. GUY

*Pastor of Friendship Baptist Church
Atlanta, Georgia*

For to every one who has will more be given, . . . but from
him who has not, even what he has will be taken away.
—Matthew 25:29

But isn't this unfair? The point of Jesus' familiar parable about
the way three servants use or fail to use their talents seems clear:
the one who has will get more, but the one who has nothing will
lose even that. Yet does not this make Jesus something of a
reactionary? Doesn't this harsh pronouncement make him a
condoner of conditions that make "the rich get richer and the
poor get poorer"?

I think not. The Master here is not justifying an economic system which perpetuates social inequities. His parable, rather, illustrates what happens when we do not put to good use the potentials
that God has given each of us. The unused talent is lost; it is
taken away; it shrivels and dies. The parable illustrates the prin-
ciple of atrophy.

I ran across my first instance of severe atrophy as a boy while
thumbing through an old book about nineteenth-century India.
There was a picture of a man with a caption that stated that he
was a yogi who had raised his right arm above his head and
vowed never to lower it. The photo seemed to verify his ascetic
prowess, for it showed him with a long stump rising from his
shoulder. What was once a healthy arm, held aloft with incredible

willpower, had eventually become fixed in an upright position—a useless appendage, lifeless and atrophied.

Atrophy like that can set in in our lives. Our imagination, for example, can atrophy. No doubt the reason many cannot respond deeply to art is not that they missed a sophomore course in art appreciation but that they suffer from stunted imagination. It is lack of imagination more than ignorance of technique that prevents persons from becoming empathically involved with a piece of music, a poem, or a painting.

Children seem to suffer less than their more world-hardened elders from such atrophy of the imagination. They enter more easily into "willing suspension of belief," a prerequisite that modern critics tell us is necessary for appreciation of literary art. My ten-year-old daughter, for instance, arose extremely happy one morning. Sometime later, in relating the incident to her mother she realized the reason for her elation. The night before, she had been reading in bed a story about a blind boy who underwent eye surgery. The chapter she completed just before going to sleep ended something like this: "Johnny would be able to *see* tomorrow!" She had so thoroughly empathized with the fictionalized character that she awoke the next morning eagerly anticipating being able to see herself—and ecstatic that she could! Something seems to dull the imagination and ability to empathize as we grow older.

Atrophy can also become a condition of the mind. And we need not think merely of senility in this connection. An incident involving two elderly gentlemen shows that mental aliveness is not necessarily lost with age. The men, one ninety and the other eighty-seven, were walking in the park when an attractive young woman passed by. They paused in their conversation and watched her until she was ought of sight. As they resumed their walk, the ninety-year old said with a sigh, "Ah, to be seventy again!"

Atrophy of mind is not a matter of age, as any conscientious teacher can testify. Faced with poorly motivated students day after day, the task is to keep young minds *alive*—high school and elementary school minds that have turned off at an early age because of indifference and hostility at home, in school, on the street.

The United Negro College Fund rightly declares: "A mind is a terrible thing to waste."

I have noted such waste with particular regret on black college campuses. Admittedly, students at every kind of college may be subjected to teachers with atrophied intellects, but my concern here is about a peculiar brand of mind-atrophy with which some black students seem to suffer. I am concerned about the black student who, having defied the odds against his getting to college in the first place, is content to waste his time and to pass through the college experience with an undeveloped mind. I am concerned about the black student who confesses openly his desire for a high-salaried job immediately upon graduation, but is unwilling to undergo the mental preparation that will enable him to qualify for it. I wonder about the black student who is quick to condemn an older generation of blacks for their naiveté and softness, but in his shallowness reveals a woeful ignorance of the history of his own people. I question the sincerity of the black student who can rattle off revolutionary phrases, but who has little conception of the depth and power of mental development and change.

There is, further, a "cool" type of student on the black campus whose very coolness works against the expansion of his mind. Don Lee has written a poem about a brother who was so cool that he was

> Super-Cool
> Ultrablack
> . . . triple-hip
>
> . . . .
> Cool-cool so cool him nick-named refrigerator.*

One might add in reference to a certain type of student: *Him so cool, his mind is atrophied!*

Atrophied minds are plentiful in the church, of course. Or to put it another way, church is often a place where "the mind has been left at the doorstep." Despite the mindlessness that characterizes so much of church activity, however, the church of *Christ*

---

* "But He Was Cool," from Don L. Lee *Don't Cry, Scream* (Detroit: Broadside Press, 1969), p. 24.

can never be a haven for atrophied minds. Christian faith requires the highest qualities of intellect, for the church has the constant theological task to interpret the gospel message for the contemporary world.

The black church, in particular, has often been accused of theological shoddiness, the implication being that the intellect has had little part to play in black religion. But an acquaintance with the history of the black church reveals that within the basically oral tradition of black Christians, theological interpretation has been both profound and consistent. From the earliest days when the slave learned to read the Bible for himself, the thrust of his interpretation of the Word was always toward *deliverance*—deliverance of one's soul and of one's people. The so-called theology of liberation, as it is emerging today through the black church, is really an extension of the theology of freedom as it was first pronounced by the antebellum black preacher. The mainstream of the black church has consistently related the biblical word to the world, here and now.

Christian commitment, therefore, does not encourage an atrophied mind; it demands an active one. The Christian must daily raise questions and make decisions regarding the tangled issues by which his life is surrounded: from racism to nationalism, from bombing to abortion, from building a hospital to passing a bond issue for a new sewer. Living out one's faith demands a mind that is alive. The great commandment enjoins, "Thou shalt love the Lord thy God" with all thy heart and soul, and "with all thy *mind.*"

Of all the ways that our lives may atrophy, including aesthetic and mental atrophy, it is spiritual atrophy that poses the greatest danger. To suffer spiritual atrophy is to be affected in the deepest dimension of our being. It is to suffer a gradual draining of life from the soul.

"It's none of my business! I have my own problem! I don't want to get involved!"—all are phrases with the mark of spiritual atrophy. Perhaps we have grown too accustomed to police beatings and crime statistics. Perhaps we have become too inured to violence by reports of daily muggings or by our favorite dramas on television. Perhaps we have dropped too many bombs on too many villages too many miles away to know that war is close-up suffering. Maybe too much evil around us has caused the warmth of life to drain from our soul. Jesus forewarned his disciples: "Because iniquity shall abound, the love of many shall wax cold."

The implications of Jesus' parable of the talents are clear: as an arm can atrophy from lack of use, so can the spirit. The spirit that does not enter into prayer will soon show signs of atrophy. The spirit that is not rejuvenated by worship will soon begin to degenerate. The spirit that does not reach out to others in active love and concern will soon find itself a hardened, lifeless appendage. The spirit must be exercised in faith.

A physician will often prescribe exercise in the form of physical therapy to offset the threat of atrophy in a bedridden or paralyzed patient. Such therapy can be painful and may demand of the patient great determination. Exercising our faith can also be like this. Sometimes it is painful to overcome our fear and to stand up—with others or alone—for what *ought* to be. It is painful to learn to give and to *for*give. It is painful to reach out with a Jesus-kind-of-love and to accept, willingly, the enmity that is often meted out in return.

Yes, the exercise of faith is sometimes painful. It is difficult because atrophy has already affected our soul. That is why the faithful pray with the Master, "Father, into thy hands I commend my spirit." For when atrophy sets in, only God can effect a cure. Only he can rebend the stiffened joints, as it were, restore the wasted tissue, and cause the life-giving blood to flow again.

May it please God to give us life and keep atrophy from setting in in our soul.

"FORWARD MARCH! WE SEE NO ALPS"

LEON H. SULLIVAN

Minister of Zion Baptist Church
Philadelphia, Pennsylvania

In Psalm 66 we find these words: "Blessed be God, which hath not turned away my prayer, nor his mercy from me." I want to talk about the central crisis facing our nation, about the basic cause of our mounting unrest and all our domestic troubles.

I can assure you, first, that the central crisis is not presently economic. Americans have never had it so good. We are enjoying a standard of living never experienced before by any people anywhere in the history of the world. Even the Roman citizen at the zenith of a flourishing empire was a piker by comparison. Never before has a population anywhere had so much economic affluence and power. And the future seems even brighter. This nation is on the threshold of a golden era of production and income and jobs and all the necessary things that make the economic wheel go around. God has blessed us as a people in an extraordinary way. Too bad we do not thank him or praise him enough for it.

Nor is the crisis facing America a crisis of politics. It seems that we are forever caught up in or on the verge of an election campaign. The Republicans tell us to elect a Republican or the nation will go to the dogs, and the Democrats tell us to elect a Democrat or things will go from bad to worse. What neither group tells us is that, whichever party wins, the taxpayer is still going to have to shell out a whole lot of tax money for the party in power. But let me be bold to say that, really and truly, it is almost impossible these days to tell the difference between a Democrat and a

Republican, and whichever slate wins we seem to want to throw them out at the next opportunity. Fortunately, we have safeguards within the structure of government to insure the continuance of the republic, whoever is elected. This is the genius of our democracy, and we can thank God for that.

Nor is the crisis facing our nation racial. This is an unbelievable statement coming from me, what with all the racial unrest and discord and hysteria and trouble in the land. How can Leon Sullivan say something like that? But, my friends, it is true. The race problem is a disturbing perplexity and will be for some time. Still, it is not the central crisis. If the problem of color were resolved today, the central crisis would remain—or else the Korean people would never have been at war with the Korean people; there was no color in that. Or the Vietnamese would never have been at war with the Vietnamese; there was no color in that. Or the inhabitants of Central Europe would not have slaughtered each other in bloody wars for a thousand years; there was no color in that.

No, the crisis goes deeper than color. As disturbing as this problem is, with all of its ramifications, the race problem is only a part, a big part, but only a part of the central crisis. Nor is the real crisis an ideological one, between the East and the West, the capitalists and the communists, for in the long stream of history all of these will be recorded as ripples on the great waves of time. The central crisis facing our nation, and indeed the whole world, is a crisis of the human spirit. It is rooted in man's heart and has to do with man's relationship with his God. Ever since the garden of Eden, man has turned his back on God by choice, and will never resolve that basic crisis in this world until, by choice, he turns back to God again. It is from this root in the soil of sin that all other evil deeds have grown. Therefore, men must be reconciled with their God if they are ever to find peace again. And this is what is so important about church: here men and women come hoping to find reconciliation with God and, in doing so, peace again.

So then, on the broader scale, in order to meet the central crisis, there are some things that we must go back for if we are

to find the peace of God that we are all consciously or uncon-
sciously seeking. It is told in the Scripture how, on one occasion,
Mary and Joseph on their return trip from Jerusalem were looking
for Jesus, and, not finding him, they had to go back to Jerusalem
to get him before they could continue their journey home. So we
must go back to the gospel of Jesus Christ for the things we have
left behind, in order that we can then move forward in the building of a better world.

We must go back to the gospel of Jesus Christ and realize that
there is something that is eternally sacred about all human life,
that a human life is the most sacred thing on earth. We are all
born in the likeness and image of God, and every man has a little
bit of God inside of him. Some call it the spirit, and some the
soul, but whatever it is called, it is this little bit of God in us that
makes the rest of us of any value at all. Man does not exist because of his legs; his legs simply carry him about. A man does
not exist because of his brain; the brain only tells him what to do.
A man does not exist because of his eyes; his eyes merely show
him where to go. Man doesn't even exist because of his heart; he
is more than his heart—he needs his heart but you can take one
heart out and put another one in. A man exists on this earth
because of the little bit of God that is in him that we call spirit or
soul. The human body is only a shelter to house that little bit of
God. Every man is sacred to God. In fact, all of life has value to
God.

Next, we must go back to Christ and his teachings, and recognize the worth of human personality. The junior chamber of com-
merce has a slogan that earth's great treasure lies in human
personality; and this is as clear as I could ever say it. We who
are affluent, who stand outside the trouble zones of our cities,
must find a new description for human potential. A boy does not
have to be white to be bright; or born in a good home to have
character; or taught in a first-class school to be educated. You
would be amazed to know the brilliance and character and genius
that prejudice has left behind, imprisoned within the trouble zone.

All the people want is a chance to prove what they can do. At
the Opportunities Industrialization Center (OIC) in Philadelphia I

have seen 10,000 men and women in that one city prove what they can do. They have been written off as untrainable, undesirable, unambitious, content with relief for a livelihood; but we took those people, gave them a massive injection of self-confidence, and helped them to know what God could do in their lives. We taught them that a man is like a balloon: it is not his color that makes him rise but what he has inside of him. What we need to do is get the color out of our eyes and to see a person as a child of God, for earth's great treasure lies in human personality, not the color of a man's skin, or where he came from. For it is not as important where a man came from as where, with God's help, he can go; not what he was, but what he can be.

Finally, we must go back to the gospel of Jesus Christ and teach men and preach to men about the power of the word of God. Sociology is of value, psychology is of value, astrology is of value, but only by theology—by God at work in the affairs of man. It is by the foolishness of preaching that the world will be saved—yes, by teaching and preaching of the word of God. For the gospel is the power of God unto salvation to every man that believeth. And remember this: the word of God is the only provision God has made for the salvation of the world and the redemption of mankind; and however many the critics of the church and of the Bible, the word of God will survive. The Bible is God's word and it is God's way. No one will ever destroy the word of God, or its power to stay in the world, or in the universe. When men are living on the moon they will be reading the word of God.

Hitlerism could not destroy it. Communism cannot destroy it. Materialism cannot destroy it. Humanism will not destroy it. Technology cannot destroy it. Space will not destroy it. Nothing can destroy it. For God's word is as indestructible as beauty, goodness, and truth. Water cannot drown it. Fire cannot burn it. Swords cannot cut it up. Bombs cannot blow it up. Prisons cannot imprison it. No cross can crucify it. No grave can hold it. The word of God is sure, enduring forever. So I say to you, pass on the word of God. If God's word has helped you, pass it on, and live by it faithfully in your day by day associations with your fellowman.

See all men as your brothers, made in the likeness and image of God. See men in terms of what they can be, not in terms of our prejudices, what we have thought they are. Above all, hold high in word and in precept and in deed the word of God, knowing that the word of God can change the world. Impossible, you say? With God, nothing is impossible.

The story is told of Hannibal, the Carthaginian general who led 50,000 men with 100 elephants along a new pass on the way to battle the Romans. His troops traveled and traveled, until at last they arrived at a place where the mountains were so high that they had never been traveled before. Hannibal, on his trusty horse shouted back to his ruffled troops in a loud voice, "Behold the Alps!" Rank by rank his words were carried back, "Behold the Alps!" A second time, Hannibal shouted to his troubled troops, "Behold the Alps!" and they echoed the cry. Then a third time Hannibal's voice rang out, "Behold the Alps!" and the third time his words were repeated rank by rank. Finally, pulling his sword from its sheath and pointing it forward for all to see, Hannibal cried out to his troops so that all could hear, "Forward march! We see no Alps!"

Facing the Alps of sin, out of which has come race prejudice and war and tyranny and materialism, it seems all too formidable for us to overcome. We are bewildered by the immensity of the obstacle. But with God as our helper, one day we shall overcome. "Forward march! We see no Alps!"

THINGS ARE NOT ALWAYS WHAT THEY SEEM

HERBERT O. EDWARDS, SR.

Associate Professor of Black Church Studies
Duke Divinity School
Durham, North Carolina

Our text is the story of Sodom and Gomorrah, and of how Lot was saved from their awful destruction (Genesis 19:1–26).

The first scene which arrests our attention is one of quietness and peace. It is evening. A fair city lies upon the border of a plain that looks like a garden in beauty and fertility. Laborers are coming in from the vineyards and fields nearby, and shepherds are settling down with their flocks on the distant hills for another peaceful night. There are no signs of trouble in the air, no indication that the wrath of God might fast be approaching. And yet the last night is casting its long shadows upon the walls of the doomed city. Things are not always what they seem. Appearances can be deceiving.

According to the custom of the land and of the time, the chief men are sitting in the gate. Old and young are abroad in the open air. The idle multitude are coming and going to gather the gossip of the day and enjoy the cool wind that comes up from the lake beyond the walls.

The people of this city have a reputation for going to every excess in indulgence. They have everything that the sensual can desire, and their only study is to find new ways of gratifying their passions.

Two strangers are seen approaching the city. They seem to be only common travelers coming down from the hill-country and turning in for shelter for the night, that they may rise up early in the morning to go on their journey refreshed. Only one man paid attention to them. Lot did not know who they were, nor did he suspect the awful errand upon which they had come. But he treated them with courtesy and respect: "Behold now, my lords, turn in, I pray you, into your servant's house, and tarry all night, and wash your feet, and ye shall rise up early, and go on your ways."

The idle throng in the streets deride the hospitable old man for taking the two strangers home to his own house. The masses are much more ready to treat the pair with rudeness and contempt. A crowd gathers outside Lot's house, demanding that he send the strangers out so that they might have some sport with them. The people themselves did not think this unusual; apparently they had done as much many times before. But there is a point beyond which the patience of God cannot go. Lot refused their request, and when the mob clamored outside Lot's door a sudden blindness fell upon them, and they did not realize that they had already passed "the hidden boundary between God's patience and his wrath."

This night seemed no different from any other. No trumpet of wrath has shattered the stillness; no earthquake has shaken the hills; no threatening wave has rolled upon the shore of the peaceful lake; no cloud of vengeance darkens the coming day. But things are not always what they seem.

Nations and individuals tend to believe that they see no evidence of approaching doom, that because God does not seem to be doing any more today that he did on days an weeks gone by they can continue in the old way. So often we fail to see the gathering clouds of disaster until they are overhead ready to rain down trouble.

The history of our country is a case in point. Thomas Jefferson once said, in commenting on the slavery in which he was also heavily involved: "I tremble for my country when I recall that God is just." But neither he nor the country was sufficiently impressed with the justice of God to do anything about slavery. So President Abraham Lincoln was to say some sixty years later: "Fondly do we hope, fervently do we pray, that this mighty scourge of war may speedily pass away. Yet, if God wills that it continue until all the wealth piled by the bondsman's two hundred and fifty years of unrequited toil shall be sunk, and until every drop of blood drawn with the lash shall be paid by another drawn with the sword, as was said three thousand years ago, so still it must be said, The judgments of the Lord are true and righteous altogether."

How often we go on our way ignoring God because he does not seem to be interfering with our activities. "Why sayest thou, O Jacob, and speakest, O Israel, My way is hid from the Lord, and my judgment is passed over from my God? Hast thou not known? hast thou not heard, that the everlasting God, the Lord, the Creator of the ends of the earth, fainteth not, neither is weary? there is no searching of his understanding."

In the winter of 1955, an insignificant and unimportant woman took a seat on a city bus in Montgomery, Alabama. Rosa Parks was not known beyond her immediate circle of family and friends, and her continued insignificance was assured by the color of her skin. When the bus driver asked her to give up her seat to a white man, the bus driver never dreamed that something was about to happen that would change the course of this nation's history. He was only doing what he had done on so many previous occasions. Why should this time be any different? But things are not always what they seem.

What happened in Montgomery, Alabama on that fateful day in 1955 might well have been God's way of giving this country another chance to redeem itself and purge itself, to repent, to make amends, and to be saved. But few were sensitive enough to receive and understand the message, and subsequent opportunities too have been largely ignored.

The messengers to Sodom give Lot the privilege of going out and urging his sons-in-law to flee from the doomed city. He makes his way to their houses through the blinded rabble in the streets and gives the warning. But he seems to them as one that is a madman. They cannot think it possible that he is in his right mind, to be coming to them at that late hour of the night with such an alarming message. They will sleep on till morning, and tomorrow they will laugh at the kindhearted old father about his midnight call.

Dawn begins to break for the doomed city. The morning star shines with its customary brightness over the mountains of Moab. The cool air, mingled with the perfume of flowers, comes up like refreshing incense from the placid sea, and the song of birds welcomes the returning light. There is nothing to fear—except that one word of the angels: "The Lord will destroy this city." The beautiful skies speak peace and safety. The sleeping city dreams of long life and continued pleasure. The coming day looks down from the eastern hills with a smile. But the angels have said: "The Lord will destroy this city!" All seems the same as the day before. But the hour of doom has come; desolation befalls a city . . .

And God made this great desolation in his own beautiful and glorious work because the sin of Sodom was great and the cry of its iniquity had come up to heaven. The last night, as serene and beautiful as ever, hung its starry curtain over a sleeping world. And when the golden dawn broke into day the rising sun had not seen in all the gorgeous East a fairer city than Sodom. Then suddenly, in one moment, her last cry went up to heaven amid tempests of fire that rained down from above and fountains of fire that burst up from the deep, and Sodom was gone. Sodom—its name had become a symbol of infamy for all generations, and now its awful doom stands forth as a perpetual sign that God's patience with sin has a point beyond which it will not go.

Every nation, every group, every individual is ever listening to two words; one is from man and the other is from God. One says: "Tarry, be at ease, enjoy yourself while you can." The other says: "Escape for your life." The one says: "Wait, be not alarmed." The other says: "Make haste, look not behind thee, flee to the mountain lest thou be consumed." One says: "Soul, take thine ease, eat, drink, and be merry." The other says: "Thou fool, this night thy soul may be required of thee." Things are not always what they seem.

There is another side of the coin. There is a tendency to lose faith in God and to despair of hope for change when it seems that all the power is on the side of wrong and injustice, when it seems that all is lost.

Peter and the apostles had left their occupations, given up their normal pursuits, and placed their faith and hope in the teachings and promises of Jesus of Nazareth. He had told them many times that he had to leave them, that the Son of man must suffer many things. But they would not hear of it. Now on this fateful evening, with his disciples gathered around the table, Jesus' words fall like a trip-hammer on their spirits, crushing their dreams, challenging again their commitment to him: "One of you is going to betray me!"

The act is done. The guards have taken him away, the court is convened, the decision rendered. The sentence is pronounced: "Crucify him!" Now all is surely lost. The disciples scatter, propelled by their fear, overwhelmed by their grief, distraught in their disappointment: "We had thought that he was the one to redeem Israel!"

All appears to be over: the broken body is buried. The tomb is securely sealed. The guards are posted. And faith and hope are buried with the corpse. But God, who always reserves the last word unto himself, immobilizes the guards, breaks the seal, removes the stone, relativizes the finality of death, and raises Jesus from the dead.

Things are not always what they seem. . . .

THE CHURCH AMID CRISIS

CHARLES E. BLAKE

*Minister of West Angeles Church of God in Christ
Los Angeles, California*

Since its origin, the church has always been confronted by various kinds of crises. During my days as a theological student in Atlanta, Georgia, the civil rights struggle was a crisis which engulfed not only the church, but all Americans.

For us students, Martin Luther King, Jr. was our role model, and we saw ourselves then and in the future as the liberators and shackle-breakers of our people. We felt that the church's greatest role was leadership of the nonviolent effort to liberate our people from economic and political oppression. We felt that once the enemies of freedom saw our Christian love their passion for violence and blood would subside; they would willingly give us our rights and accept us as brothers. But our love was not potent enough to transform their hearts: bombs still went off in churches, snipers' bullets still came out of the darkness, stones and sticks still beat us to the ground. And so, the nonviolent vernacular was washed away by a flood of militant rhetoric; and brotherhood, by pride and nationalism.

The church, shocked by its loss of leadership, and by its sudden alienation from the most vocal segments of society, searched for other banners under which to march. We jumped on everybody's bandwagon. We sought to be relevant. We defined and evaluated ourselves by the kinds of causes we supported and the institutional programs we offered.

The church's traditional concept of the ministry was broadened to stress less its religious orientation and more its social and economic orientation. But these programs dealt only with the *symptoms of the problem*; they could not reach the source. Very few people now find purpose, meaning, or fulfillment within our social system.

Dean Kelley, author of *Why Conservative Churches Are Growing,* asserts that man is "an inveterate meaning-monger—a meaning-oriented being." The crisis which faces the church and the world is what Kelley calls "the malady of the absence of meaning." When the individual cannot make sense out of his existence, he may become embittered and despairing, then listless and parasitic, or erratic, violent, "criminal,"—even suicidal. This is what faces us today. Dean Kelley says that "a culture which cannot stand on its world of shared meanings through time will not survive." It is "the indispensable function of religion" to provide man with understanding of the ultimate meaning of life. Kelley refers to Yinger's definition of religion as "a system of beliefs and practices by means of which a group of people struggle with these ultimate problems of human life."*

Every day there are church people who, having given themselves to some mistress, some alternative involvement which separates them from the true mate of their souls, some dissipating endeavor which renders them incapable of performing their primary responsibilities—every day there are church people, standing on the bridge of life, who pass by suffering, anxious, frustrated, desperate, and hopeless humanity. As these church people pass along the way, they hear the horrifying splash of a suicidal humanity falling into the harsh waters of destruction. Yet they are immobilized by their own fear, frenzy, and ignorance, their sense of powerlessness and lostness as they hear the desperate shrieks of humanity going down for the last time. And then, totally exhausted by the thought of what they could have done, or should have done, they stumble away talking to themselves.

And as they walk away they remind us of the two men who left convulsive Calvary and started walking toward Emmaus. Not

---

* Dean Kelley, *Why Conservative Churches Are Growing* (New York: Harper & Row, 1972), pp. 38–41.

knowing the significance of the Cross, they contemplated the supposed failures of the past, wrestled for a doctrine of history that would explain their present, and grappled for a theory that would give meaning to their future. A Stranger walked beside them, waiting for their eyes to open.

It may sound simplistic and naive, but the root cause of man's dilemma, is sin. Behind our loss of meaning, behind our self-destructiveness and hostility, behind our crisis stands our sin. We sinfully declared our independence from God. We sought to order and sustain our existence by ourselves, and by our own standards. As a result, we became separated from God. The evil and destructiveness of human nature came to the fore. Men became hateful and hostile toward one another. Having lost reality, they began to chase after empty dreams. Having forsaken the truth, they were dependent on meaningless theories.

There is no human or earthly technique for dealing with sin. We may strive to meet the sinner's physical and intellectual needs, but still we have not dealt with his basic condition. God has provided an indispensable means of dealing with sin. The Apostle Paul said, "This is a faithful saying and worthy of all acceptation, that Christ Jesus came into the world to save sinners" (1 Tim. 1:15).

Jesus Christ came to bring life and meaning unto men. He died on a cross to show the extent of God's love, and to suffer the penalty that you and I deserve to suffer. He died that men might be reunited with God. But, he also rose from the dead, and he still lives today. Those who accept him personally into their lives have found freedom and forgiveness. They have been delivered from the things that pulled them down. They have a faith that no tragedy or problem can destroy. They have been delivered from hangs-ups that could not be dealt with on the human level. Because he lives, they look forward to the joys of eternal life. They have a contentment and satisfaction that nothing on earth can provide.

Every once in a while we need to be called back to basics. The greatest single need of our day is for the gospel of Jesus Christ: "God so loved the world, that he gave his only begotten Son, that whosoever believeth in him should not perish, but have everlasting life" (John 3:16). "As many as received him, to them gave he power to become the sons of God" (John 1:12). "Therefore if any man be in Christ, he is a new creature: old things are passed away; behold, all things are become new" (2 Cor. 5:17).

Where do we go from here? Let's go back to basics. Let these truths be the foundation of every discipline. Let them be the essence of our preaching. "It pleased God by the foolishness of what we preach to save them that believe" (1 Cor. 1:21).

Tell it. Tell it from house to house. Tell it from door to door. Tell it to the unfair employer, and the word of God will do more than a strike ever could. Tell it to that "street woman," and the word of God will strip her of the symbols of her profession and clothe her in the apparel of respectability. Tell it to that addict, and Jesus will take him higher than he has ever been before. Tell it to that hypocritical white man who claims to know Christ, but in reality doesn't know Christ at all. Tell it to the mayor who may have forgotten that "except the Lord keep the city, the watchman waketh but in vain." Tell it to the politician and the man of military might, for "when a man's ways please the Lord, he maketh even his enemies to be at peace with him." Tell it! Tell it to that black militant, for with Christ in his heart he is more powerful than he could ever be with a Molotov cocktail in his hand. During these days of crisis we must not forget our primary responsibility—preach the word!

THE LIMITATIONS OF GOD'S POWER

OSWALD P. BRONSON

*President of Bethune-Cookman College
Daytona Beach, Florida*

There are at least five things that God cannot do. Of course, it sounds almost heretical to talk about what God cannot do, because this seems to go against the very nature and attributes of God.

The "omnipotence" of God, for example, as traditionally understood, refers precisely to his power to do everything. It also refers to God's sovereignty and independence. The Christian doctrine of creation speaks of an all-powerful God who created the totality of the cosmic process. By his omnipotence God spoke and the planetary systems came forth; the sun shone, the wind blew, and everything around us came into being. But, in spite of all God's majestic power, there are five things that he cannot do.

Well, what about the "omnipresence" of God? Not only is God all powerful, but his omnipresence means that he is everywhere at the same time. He interpenetrates everything in his imminence. His presence is with the most infinitesimal aspect of reality, as well as the most complex. God is also beyond the world, meaning that he is transcendent. The omnipresence of God further substantiates his unqualified omnipotence. And yet, there are five things God cannot do.

Another attribute of God that is inextricably bound up with his omnipotence and omnipresence is his "omniscience," which refers to the fact that God knows everything. He knows each of us better than we know ourselves. He knows even the hairs of our heads; he knows our thoughts and he knows our days. But, in spite of all these qualities that describe the inexhaustible power of God, the paradox remains: there are five things that God cannot do.

God's unqualified power has been demonstrated through the ages. It was demonstrated in the life of Israel. God delivered the Israelites out of Egypt. The biblical narratives portray God as the deliverer. In addition to God's delivering power there is his healing power, for he said, "I am the Lord thy God that healeth thee." God heals through physicians and medicine as well as through spiritual and other means. Thus, in view of the wonderful things that God does and is capable of doing, it becomes increasingly difficult even to entertain the thought that there are some things that God cannot do.

Jesus himself said, "With God all things are possible." Should I then doubt or debate with Jesus? No, because Jesus would agree about the five things God cannot do:

First, God cannot lie, because God is truth. Jesus reflected on this when he said, "I am the truth, the way, and the life." For God to lie would be to go against his nature, and he cannot do that. God and his word are firm, infinite, unchanging, eternal, and infallible. Man can always depend on God. This is the truth that will have the final word in reality. It is the truth that, though knocked to the ground, will rise again. Truth is intrinsically a part of God and, therefore, opposed to all lies. God cannot lie.

Second, God cannot make a mistake. The problem of evil challenges this statement. If God makes no mistakes, then how are we to explain the presence of evil in the world and in human affairs? There is an explanation for the presence of evil in human relations, though the presence of natural evils such as earthquakes, storms, tornadoes, famines, and pestilence will probably always remain an unexplainable mystery. In human relations evil is among us quite simply because we hate when we should love. We have not dealt rightly in terms of justice, equality, righteousness, and respect for the value and worth of human life. And when there is a crisis in human affairs we blame God for it, whereas we are our own problem. God will not do for man what man is capable of doing for himself, and God will not force man into doing what man doesn't want to do. God doesn't violate the freedom and responsibility of mankind. No, God cannot make a mistake; it is *man* who makes the mistakes.

Third, God cannot save us unless we find the oneness that he gave us. Divided against each other we cannot "make it." Jesus admonished, "A house divided against itself cannot stand," and in the garden of Gethsemane he prayed, "Father, make them one as we are one." Unless we find this unity that God has given us, we will not stand and we will not be saved.

Fourth, God cannot stop loving us. God is love. His nature is love, and everything he does is love. "For God so loved the world that he gave his only begotten son, that whosoever believeth in him shall not perish, but have everlasting life." We might stop loving him, but God cannot stop loving us; his love for us shall last forever. Man tends to hate the sinner and love the sin, but God hates the sin and loves the sinner.

Fifth, God cannot die. If he did die, then he would cease to be God. Time consists of perpetual perishing. Reality consists of both being and becoming, a dialectical process involving both birth and death. All life is finite, temporal, and transitory, but God transcends finitude, temporality, and transciency. God in his imminence is caught up in the perpetually ongoing becomingness of reality, and in this way he sustains man and attempts to influence man toward the attainment of the good. God in his transcendence is beyond and above the transitories of life. Because of this, God is both the realization and the conservation of value. He abides.

God cannot lie, God cannot die; he cannot make a mistake. God cannot save us unless we find the oneness that he gave us. And we *will* find it, because God cannot stop loving us. Yes, there is much that God cannot do—because he remains true to his nature. And it is precisely because of these special "limitations" that we can give thanks and trust in him. They are what make him "our help in ages past, our hope for years to come."